To my friend:

Here's hoping this work will be a blessing to you and that you can share it with anyone you know who might be needful of the message. I'll always remember this day of reunion in Surfside Beach, S.C. Thanks, dear Gordon, for the memories and wonderful companionships.

Forever closest friend,

Joseph Anthony. 6/28/07

The Alabaster Boy

by

Joseph Anthony

authorHOUSE

1663 LIBERTY DRIVE, SUITE 200
BLOOMINGTON, INDIANA 47403
(800) 839-8640
www.authorhouse.com

© 2004 Joseph Anthony
All Rights Reserved.

No part of this book may be reproduced, stored in a retrieval system, or transmitted by any means without the written permission of the author.

First published by AuthorHouse 04/01/04

ISBN: 1-4184-0153-6(e)
ISBN: 1-4184-0154-4 (sc)

Printed in the United States of America
Bloomington, Indiana

This book is printed on acid-free paper.

THANKSGIVING TO MY GOD

"Come unto Me, all you who labor and are heavy-laden and over burdened, and I will cause you to rest your minds, spirits and bodies. You will find *relief, refreshment, recreation* and *blessed quiet* for your tormented minds (souls)". (Matthew, chapter 11, verses 28-29)

DEDICATION

To my beloved wife: Margaret, who is the reason I began writing and continue to write better. She has been and always will be my guide to excellence in all that matters in life.

IN RECOGNITION

This work I now present is for everyone who has suffered physical, sexual or emotional pain at the hands of others, as I have. It is my way of helping to not only ease those pains, but to eradicate the memories of shame, degradation or violence that were ***not,*** repeat, ***not*** your fault. After sharing my life with you, I hope you too will think only the best about yourself. This is my hug to the world. Goodbye for now. Will write to you again soon,

Joseph Anthony

TABLE OF CONTENTS

CHAPTER 1—ROOTS OF ABUSE 1

CHAPTER 2—OF HUMAN BONDAGE 15

CHAPTER 3—THE ALABASTER BOY 32

CHAPTER 4—JOURNEY TO THE PROMISED LAND 56

CHAPTER 5—A ROSE GREW AMONG THE LILACS 70

CHAPTER 6—OUT OF CONTROL 90

CHAPTER 7—ON THE YARD 110

CHAPTER 8—THE GAUNTLET 122

CHAPTER 9—MARITAL ABUSE 136

CHAPTER 10—VEGAS-THE OPENING ACT 152

CHAPTER 11—VEGAS-THE CLOSING ACT 162

CHAPTER 12—SPIRITUAL AND CLINICAL HEALING 174

PROLOGUE

"Backward, turn backward, O Time, in your flight,
Make me a child again just for tonight"!

Elizabeth Akers Allen's 'Rock Me to Sleep' - 1860

CHAPTER 1—ROOTS OF ABUSE

My brother: Johnny, *tried* to fire the semi-automatic handgun, but it jammed. My eager hands grabbed the gun, cleared the chamber, pointed at Jamie's car and emptied the gun, sending messengers of death ripping through the door panels and shattering the passenger window. Bluish - white flames screamed out of the muzzle at the same time, shattering the silence of an early afternoon in Las Vegas. Staring in disbelief, I watched the gold Lincoln Continental speed off with Jamie still alive. I was furious, to put it mildly. I was in a rage!

Joseph Anthony

Within minutes, three Metro squad cars and part of the homicide department arrived and questioned Johnny, Debbie and me. Debbie used to be one of Jamie's working girls, but he took her off the streets and kept her as his *main squeeze.* We were all taken downtown, but released for insufficient evidence because we all stuck to the same story: Jamie pulled up and opened fire on us. "If that's true, where are *Jamie's* shell casings? We found all of *your's* with a metal detector", the detective said. "Jamie uses a revolver. The shells stay in a revolver. Even a rookie knows that", I answered. "You three are free to go", he said, "but if anything unfortunate befalls Jamie…we'll be talking again."

A uniformed policeman drove us back to our apartment, where Debbie and I spent the next three days and nights in steamy passion, desperately trying to escape what we were: her, a washed-up prostitute and me, a 31 year old has-been boxer. "How did I ever get this way", I wondered one night? "I didn't start out this way". Memories of post W.W.II haunted me until I went back in time to confront the torment and find out just how it *did* begin and was allowed to grow.

Scottie screamed loudly with each contraction growing closer and more intense. Soon Mama's neighbor and midwife: Rosie, helped me into this cold world on the morning of October 12, 1946. The country doctor arrived later, put a drop of silver nitrate in each of my eyes and said, "mark my words, this boy will prove to be very strong and wiry if given the chance". He had stood in the same spot twice before, when my brothers: Edmund, Jr. and Johnny were born, and had been called to the house at other times to patch up Scottie or Edmund, Sr. after one of their many fights.

My first few years were spent by Rosie's and Mama's side, in a made-over tarpaper shack my father had fashioned upon 125 acres of land. Somehow, he forced that barren patch of dirt to yield to him, bringing forth wheat, bell peppers, corn, beans, oranges, lemons and watermelons.

Edmund also forced Rosie to yield to him, bringing forth sexual favors. Both satisfied each other's needs, on those nights when Mama went to the small town of Escondido, drinking and finding her own sexual and emotional needs met. This, my father revealed to me when I was in my early twenties, adding a more graphic description to his exploits. "The only time Rosie turned me down was during her period. Do you know what a woman's period is", he asked? "Yes, Dad, I've been married for a year and a half", I answered. "Well I told her that blood didn't bother me, but she was stubborn. She was too stupid to know that men like to see their women bleed. He didn't have to convince me. Mama and I were living testimonies of his strange lust for blood and violence. Don't get me wrong. Edmund, Sr. was not a madman, but was cruel. It simply leapt forward from his own childhood, especially when he drank. His stepfather was also very cruel, helping to spawn a dark side that derived pleasure from loathsome

The Alabaster Boy

acts or things. In short, there was a ghoulish side to his personality, which he couldn't help.

Considering my own environment brought back thoughts of the shack in southern California. Brown, shingle siding covered the tarpaper and we did have running water. At some point Dad built a very large, 3-walled patio out of cinder blocks. I guess he thought he was building a paradise for us. A paradise without a canopy or any form of sun protection. We were only several miles from the Mexican border and *hot* was the order of the day…every day.

The post war era I was born into provided a civil service job for my father. The war itself was responsible for widespread adultery, resulting in broken homes and spur of the moment marriages. Such was the case of Scottie and Edmund. He, desperately seeking love that would help him forget the memories of a hateful childhood and her, equally desperate to find a new provider for herself and three children from a previous marriage. Their's was a love-hate relationship, but they did their very best with what they had. Everyone loves their babies. Almost everyone. Some maim or kill their babies.

Working at an army camp in the mountains, Dad was given the use of a big, green army truck: a troop transport that was powerful and very loud. Each Friday at sundown, I could hear the truck approaching from miles away. Sound carries far in the countryside. That was my signal to run to the *Highway 1 Bar* and warn Mama that he was getting dangerously close to home and she better get there quick. Standing between her and Blackie was always a hard job, because they were always wrapped around each other and I had to act like a boxing referee, trying to tear them apart, so we could get home before Edmund. "C'mon, darlin'. Blackie will get us home right quick", she said, but it was too late that night. When Blackie dropped us off, it was in back of the parked, army truck. Edmund was home and that meant trouble, violence and maybe worse.

The Alabaster Boy

Don't brand my Mama as a whore. She was not. She was a wife and mother, so rejected and severely beaten on a daily basis, that she sought escape through alcohol and affection in the arms of other men. Those who were not sadistic, jealous or inclined to murder her. What woman wouldn't succumb to a gentleman who would buy her all the drinks she needed? Drinks that helped her travel far away from Edmund's world of terror, into a world of comfort and pleasure, where some man would love her, if only for the night. Later in life drinks would also help *me* escape reality and abuse alcohol.

Blackie was a big, rotund man and always seemed happy. Children are drawn to happy people that treat them kind, so Scottie saw him as often as she could and so did I. He was nice, owned the bar and let my brothers and I play there whenever Mama visited. "Who dropped you off", Edmund demanded? "He's nice. Not like you", said Scottie. On the 3 hour drive from the mountain camp the *old man* prepared himself by downing cheap whiskey and working himself into a rage. Now he was going berserk. "OK, so he was nice, huh? See how nice you think *this* is", he screamed! A powerful right hand smashed into her cheekbone, lifting her off of the floor, throwing her against the wall. "If you think *that* felt nice, try *this* one", he growled, as his left hand slapped the other side of her face. She slid down the wall and hit the floor. Terrified, I was unable to help her. Grabbing her by the throat, he lifted her to an upright position with one hand while his other hand gripped her like a steel vice between her legs. "You dirty, lousy whore. You're trying to *make* me kill you, aren't you", he demanded? "Daddy, stop it", I screamed. "Shut up you little s.o.b. or I'll kill you too", he said in a guttural scream. He continued choking her and slamming her hips back and forth into the wall. "I took you and your 3 little bastards out of the bean fields of Texas, gave you a roof over your heads and what's more…gave you my name and respectability! And this is the thanks I get"? Scottie squeaked in a raspy voice,

The Alabaster Boy

"go ahead and kill me. It'd be better than living like this", she responded. "Oh no, I'm saving that for last. First you're gonna' give *me* what you gave him. Then I'm gonna' punch your guts out so there won't be any more little bastards showing up around here. Especially the little monster you might have in your belly after f——n' Blackie. Oh, yeh. I know who that lousy, fat hog is. I'll rip his arms off and beat him to death with the bloody stumps. Now *gimme* that…*right now*", he roared! "Please Eddie, not in front of Joey", Scottie pleaded. "What about you and Blackie in front of Joey", he countered. I suppose *that's* ok huh"? Battered and dazed, she couldn't answer, which made him even madder. His spirit and mind gave way to satanic forces, changing his voice to something half animal and half human. Now the *really* mean streak in Edmund was loosed, as if out of hell. Emotionally, he had broken down the wall of partition between madness and sanity. Grabbing her by the hair, he snarled, "all you red haired bitches are nymphomaniacs. I oughta' weld your box shut". Then in one powerful, looping, overhead toss, he flung her into the air. She cart-wheeled in mid air, landing across the room in a pathetic heap. Dear Jesus in heaven…that man could really make her fly. Looking at Mama lying helpless under the Christmas tree burned an image into my mind that has lasted all of my life. As a result, I have never laid a hand on any woman, except one who attacked me when I was eighteen. Mama was beaten almost beyond recognition, her beauty now transformed into a black and blue face with split lips and bloody nose. Tufts of red hair were ripped out of her head and were lying around on the floor. All this in her own home, supposedly a place of refuge, safety and warmth. The saddest part? She was reduced to that level by the same man who vowed to love and cherish her when they were married.

One of Scottie's children from a previous marriage was 15 year old George, who rushed in while Dad again tried to kill her. George shouted, "stop right now or I'll blow your liver out. Now get up and get out

The Alabaster Boy

cause' you ain't the big *he bull* no more". The *old man* started to make a move, but George fired a warning shot through the ceiling, then pointed the rifle at Edmund again, who promptly left with his tail tucked between his legs. This also taught me a lesson that I would use later in life, when the *old man* would once again face a younger buck, another gun and another defeat.

George said to me, "go sleep in Mama's bed. I'll take her to the hospital and she'll be alright. Go to sleep, Joey. Nobody will bother you". Unknown to me was the fact that George had already had some sort of medical training, which he learned from sailors at the San Diego Naval base. As a result, he was able to nurse Mama back to health, after tending to her immediate needs. Years later, I met George in Las Vegas and found he had been a medical coreman in Vietnam, going on to be a radiologist in an Oregon hospital. It seems that he was affected by the violence too, in a way that led him into a life of also wanting to please or help others, as I would later in life.

Joseph Anthony

Several hours later the *old man* returned to the shack. I was standing in the hallway, when the entire front door came crashing in, along with the door jams. In his meanest mood and armed with a double barreled shotgun, he met George again, who was unarmed. "So I'm not the big he-bull anymore, huh"? The *old man* said. "Now *you* get out and take Charlene and Paul. Don't ever come back". They left, but I still remember George sending me to bed that first night. I awoke to see Mama naked, examining her bruises in the mirror. She was thin, without large breasts. Her waist was thin and her hips flared gently down to her thighs. Inside of her thighs, I saw a triangle of soft looking, auburn hair. "What's that, Mama", I asked? "Oh, it's what me and Daddy were fightin' about". By this time, I was sitting up in bed. Mama put on a pink, Chenille robe and came to bed, holding me with her freshly beaten body, until all of my shaking

stopped. I put my arms around her, hoping to make the bruises go away, then fell into the safety and

The Alabaster Boy

slumber of my Mama's protection, even though short lived.

Boom! A huge hand smashed through the door, sending splinters and plaster chips across the bedroom. Then, unlocking the door through the hole he had just made, my father stomped toward us, reeling from drunkenness with a bottle of whiskey in one hand and the rifle he recaptured from George in the other. Somehow, Mama summoned up the courage to say, "please, Eddie...no more tonight. I'll put Joey in his own bed and you just relax, get undressed and come sleep in your bed". There was a lot of crying I heard from their bedroom that night. I guess they were making up. I fell asleep, dreaming about what tomorrow would bring. It arrived bringing peace, as did the next few days. Those uneventful days were welcomed, being far and few between. Perhaps that's why today

I prefer the quiet of writing, the joy of painting and the solitude of the outdoors. During my teenage and early adult years, I tried desperately to capture that elusive quiet and solitude through the use of more alcohol. Some years later I learned that being a child of alcohol dependant parents had put *me* in a high risk category for becoming an alcoholic and an abuser of some sort. Not that I *would* become one, but was a more likely candidate than others. Strike one against me was because of that and strike two due to being part of such severe domestic violence. I was being counted out in a game where I didn't have a bat and there wasn't even a referee present. In the game of life, if you get just one too many strikes, without ever being allowed to step up to the plate, you can lose the will to play and leave the stadium, convinced that *you* are to blame and *you* must pay.

CHAPTER 2—OF HUMAN BONDAGE

Soon afterward, a wonderful evening came to our house, which Mama called Christmas Eve, explaining Santa and his helpers as a kind, old man who gave toys to children once a year. Toys his helpers made. "That's why we need to put out some cookies and milk, then get in bed, so St. Nick will be quick", she quipped, unable to smile because her facial wounds would crack open and start bleeding again. Even after the initial physical abuse, victims are in a state of pain until healing is complete in their bodies, providing another beating doesn't occur first. The mental pain of guilt and fear of another assault *never* heals…unless you take *the cure.*

That evening was filled with warmth, love, tinsel and candies already under the tree, as Mama laid me in my own little army cot, to fall asleep and wait for toys. "Will Santa come if I wet my bed tonight", I asked? She always called my Joy instead of Joey because of her Texas accent.

"Now, Joy, Santa knows how good you've been and a wet bed won't make any difference, because his helpers will make everything clean, so you can wake up happy and dry. Now give Mama some sugar and go to sleep", she said.

Questions filled my mind, as I waited. There was no Easter bunny, I knew, because just about 9 months earlier I saw my half brothers and sister planting candy eggs in the back yard. Besides, rabbits didn't lay eggs… *chickens* did, because my father had a chicken coop and every morning I looked under the chickens, finding eggs

The Alabaster Boy

and bringing them inside, where Mama put them in the refrigerator. What about Santa? Was *he* real?

I'd never seen him, but Mama really must have, because she knew what he looked like and could describe his helpers. She even put out cookies and milk and I was well-drilled by my father on the great sin of wasting food, so I *knew* Mama wouldn't dare waste any. The *old man, who* is what he told us kids to call him, didn't believe in anyone except himself, so his opinion didn't count. Blackie the bar owner had his lounge decorated with wreaths, candles, lights and stockings, so *he* must have believed. My half brothers didn't believe in him either. Our *friendly* midwife and neighbor: Rosie was in the front room, drinking with Mama. "Do you think that little boy of yours knows that Santa ain't real", she asked"? Don't you ruin it for him", mama said. "I've done everything I can to make him think there's at least *one* nice person in this world. Tonight, my baby: Joy, will be happy, even if it's only for one night. You just watch my little Darlin's eyes light up when he

17

finds out Santa really came to visit him *and* left him goodies", she exclaimed. "Well, where's all these toys and goodies", asked Rosie? "Never you mind. There around here somewhere. I saved every dime I could from waitressing to buy them. Joy will have a beautiful Christmas", she answered.

That settled it for me. There was no Santa Claus, so why should I lay awake waiting for someone to visit me in the middle of the night, when he wasn't even real? Just before falling asleep, I heard Rosie say something. "Well, Scottie, maybe in a way, there's *lots* of Santa's. I've had a lot of nice men visit me in the middle of the night", she laughed. Rosie was thinking about sexual visitors and I about Santa. What she said made sense. There would have to be a lot of Santa's if they were to visit every child in the whole world in one single night. "Well, if he *is* real, I'll see him when he comes to my bedside", I thought.

The real issue was how a little boy could be so jaded; yet still hold a flickering hope, that there was indeed, a jolly old fat man with a long white beard, who brought presents to children.

Scottie's mother was a *Holiness* preacher down in Texas, so Jesus was mentioned to me occasionally. Thinking back to the night of the last beating made me recall my mother's body landing on the nativity scene my father had set-up under the tree. *Peace* on Earth? *Good* will towards men? How about good will towards *women* and *children?* The next morning I went to the Christmas tree in search of Jesus, Mary, Joseph and the wise men. They had all been smashed by the weight of my mother's body. They told me the Easter bunny was real, Santa was real and Jesus was real. Drifting off to sleep with the knowledge that Santa and the Easter bunny were fakes, I somehow smothered memories of the beating and wondered if *Jesus* was just another, whom I would discover to be a parent's lie that made kids feel good. The height of abuse is to take away the only hope left: your belief in God.

Joseph Anthony

Sometime during the night I awoke to find a very large Christmas stocking hanging on the wall above my little bed. Excited, I bolted out of the little army cot, ran to my father, grabbed him and pulled him into the bedroom. "Look", I said, "there really *is* a Santa Claus". He downplayed it with an abrupt "bull———", returning to his easy chair for a night of drinking and loneliness, while he observed Christmas Eve. How miserable he must have been: stuck with an unfaithful wife, who didn't tell him she had 3 children or an ex-husband until *after* their marriage. Even on this special night, he knew she was *honky-tonkin* down at Blackie's bar, while he recalled the good old days back in East Chicago, Indiana, thinking of his family gathered around the table, sharing good wishes good cheer and hope for the New Year, finishing with a family prayer. As I write this story, I remember him sitting solemnly, upon a very basic wooden chair, in the midst of an empty living room, clutching his whiskey bottle in one hand and wiping away the tears with the other hand. I

The Alabaster Boy

know. I was watching from the hallway that led from my bedroom.

What was he feeling? *Abuse!* He truly loved us, but couldn't show emotion, for it had been ripped out of him during his *own* childhood days. His real father died when he was two. Shortly thereafter, a new stepfather sent him and his brothers and sisters to local farms, where they picked onions for a nickel a bushel, giving all the money to grandmother, because grandpa gave them none of his, preferring to spend it on booze. So there he sat on December 24th, suffering terrible mental anguish: a product of his childhood and other forces that compelled him to pass it on to me. Hating his own actions, Edmund tried in many ways to make up for them, by being nice to us. Meanwhile, he felt worthless as a human being, so decided to slowly kill himself by drinking himself to death and almost succeeded. Mama must have been cut from the same stalk, for she did succeed. If you have any feelings at all, you can see that they added self-abuse to their own lives. If you're wounded too much or in enough pain death seems a small price to pay for relief. You develop the will to die. I am weeping now, so I must go on to someplace where there was an occasional moment of joy, or at least happiness. The same night, a few hours later, my father's big, powerful hands, nudged me ever so gently, awakening me to my second, big surprise: *another* big stocking now hung next to the first. I kissed my daddy on the cheek that night. The only other time I was allowed to do so, was years later, when I kissed him again on his cheek, as he lay in his casket. My tears hit his cheekbones but didn't seem to bother him or the undertaker's facial make-up. It bothered some people in the funeral parlor, that a 22 year old man would weep so hard over a father who had been so severe in raising me. I wasn't then, am not now and shall never be ashamed of that, for…I loved my father.

That Christmas Eve contained a lot of lessons, all of them temporarily suppressed, but not forgotten. My father told me the second stocking was bought and

The Alabaster Boy

paid for by him, saying, "will you forget about this big, stupid, fat jerk with a white beard"? "He's just like Blackie down at the bar: a big mouth, lard ass that can only impress children. *I'm* your *real* father. You come to *me* when you need something. You see all the Christmas stockings, the tree and the gifts underneath? I bought them with *my* hard earned money". I was right all along: there was nothing for nothing. You had to pay for everything you got. Even love had a price it seemed.

A few hours later, when Christmas day dawned, my beliefs would be savagely reinforced, as I paid dearly for last night's gifts. My half brothers and sister had left home, unwilling to further be pawn's in the sadistic game their parents played. That left Edmund, Jr., Johnny and me: our father's only real children from his marriage to Scottie. We all tore gleefully into the bags of candy, nuts and figs that waited under the tree, which he had repaired overnight. Old time Christmas tree lights, the kind that had colored fluid and bubbles inside, softly rose and fell, reflecting upon the silver tinsel, making the whole corner of the room light-up with happiness and flashes of light that felt like soft sponges warming your body. An angel topped the tree, soft and pure and full of goodness. Later in life, I learned that *real* angels will *protect* you! They are not blonde haired women with long white gowns, nor are they fat little naked babies buzzing around your head with little, cupid-like bows and arrows. How is a woman or naked baby going to protect a grown man? In reality, God Almighty said, *"MY* angels excel in strength and hearken unto my voice, which is my Word". Now *that's* power!

There we were like the three kings of the orient, however; at Jesus' birth were his mother and father. The absence of my mama and daddy was obvious, as we visited the broken manger. Soon they arrived and I could see that the demons within had already had their *own* holiday with Edmund and Scottie and were about to do the same with me. With Santa, the Easter Bunny and Jesus being drummed out of my life, I didn't even have God to call upon for mercy.

The Alabaster Boy

"Who ate all of the figs? Was it you three little hogs"? Then, as anger took complete control over his mind and body, his face turned red and a voice again came out of him that was half human and half animal. Like a shrieking, wounded Grizzly bear. "I was saving them for Uncle John and my mother. They're bringing polish ham and kielbosa. Now what do I have to offer them? Nothing"! We stood silent, knowing any answer would be the wrong one. We thought the figs were part of *our* Christmas. We were wrong.

"Go get the razor strap and I'll teach you to eat without my permission. I'll find out who the instigator was". Returning empty handed, we all swore that we couldn't find the strap, although we really didn't try. You see, there was no sense in trying to outwit a 35 year old war veteran. He went looking and wouldn't you know it: found it under my little army cot, which I had wet only an hour ago.

"Oh. I see *several* crimes have been committed this morning. You all know what that means", he said.

Joseph Anthony

"First I want to know who ate part of the figs". In unison, we replied, "we all did. We thought they were for us", we added. One at a time, he marched us up to him, waving that razor strap in a fashion that cut lashes on our bare bottoms.

The worst part was waiting to see who he'd call next. I was last and took the punishment for eating Christmas goodies, without one whimper, I wasn't giving in anymore. Just as he released me to join my brothers, Scottie's drunken spirit spoke out. "Oh, Eddie, did I tell you Joy pissed the bed again. What do you think his punishment should be", she asked? Edmund said, "more lashes with this razor strap". She suddenly turned on him and said, "if you touch Joy again, you'll kill him. Then I'll kill you, I swear." The old man had come to know Scottie's threats as promises, so he waltzed his way out of that one, saying, "I'll teach him a lesson without hurting him. One that you and I will *enjoy* and will probably cure him of bed-wetting", he said.

The Alabaster Boy

It was now about noon, as I stood completely naked in the front room, with my flour sack shorts dropped around my ankles, awaiting further punishment. The *old man* fashioned a note that read, "*Joey is a piss pot*", then, twisted it in opposite directions at each end, so it would resemble one of those party poppers. Tying a string to the middle of it and the other end of the string to my penis…all was ready. "Now, stick your thumb in your mouth and start marching around the room until I say stop". He shouted, "forward…march"! The old grandfather clock chimed twelve times, as if to signal the commencement of my macabre march around the *old man's* personal parade ground.

Mother and father looked upon me, as they downed each successive drink. The problem was they could drink for hours. What they didn't know was that I could march for hours and outlast them, as young as I was. The *old man* knew precisely what he was doing in making the apparatus now tied to me and making me leave my little shorts wrapped around my ankles.

Joseph Anthony

It made me walk as a prisoner in hobbles, in an erratic, jerking motion. With each step my little penis bobbed up and down making the note on the other end dance up and down when it hit the floor. Suddenly he slammed his fist on the table, demanding, "when are you gonna' stop pissin' in the bed"? Unable to answer I just stood there looking at the floor. *"Answer me"*, he yelled, "or I'll rip that little pecker of yours off at the roots. You make me so mad I could kill you right now, you no good little c___s___r"! My only possible response was to keep sucking my thumb and keep my cadence, as I watched him grind his teeth, so full of rage he couldn't speak any further. He often snapped into a different kind of person for no apparent reason. The old grandfather clock now chimed four times. I was learning how to tell time. It was four hours after the clock first chimed.

Just then, Uncle John tapped upon the front door and without waiting, entered with grandma, announcing, "knock-knock and Merry Christmas", in a cheerful voice. From the bedroom I was sent to, I heard

The Alabaster Boy

him ask, "Hey Ed, why weren't you at the airport to pick us up? We took a taxi all the way from San Diego". The answer was obvious, as the *old man,* in a semi-stupor, answered, "not that it's any of your business, but I was instructing Joey on how to be a man". Bushia (grandma in Polish) asked, "so where is my grandson"? The *old man* shouted, "Joey, come out here." Uncle John and Bushia were horrified at their first look at me. "Ed, what in the world is going on here? Lessons in manhood, huh? Why, he's only a baby. What could he possibly have done to deserve *this* kind of treatment"? Bushia was shouting into the *old man's* face. Her old heart was broken to know that they had walked in on the truth of how things were, quite different from her son's letters. Uncle John picked me up, carried me to my bed, talked softly and cleaned me up, presenting me again to my parents. "Now *this* is how Joey should look", he proudly announced. "A horse's ass is what you are, John. You don't know what that kid's done", the *old man* responded. "Well", said Uncle John, "one of these days this baby's going to grow up. When he does, you better pray he doesn't remember any of this"...but I did.

Later in life, I deeply identified with Jesus. They beat *Him*, stripped *Him* naked and humiliated *Him* too, yet He was innocent. I do not think I'm Jesus or God, nor do I have any sort of messianic complex. I felt guilty as the cause of my own punishment. Putting that type of guilt trip on a child is the act of a *monster.* It takes *years* for some of us to recover.

Pleading for some sort of explanation, Uncle John asked Scottie, "Do you go along with this? You're their mother. Don't you care"? She answered spitefully: "You Polacks are self-righteous and hate me cause' I'm a hillbilly. Well let me tell *you* a thang or two. My old man is the head of this clan and whot he says is law. When I git my southern blood up, Ah'll go anywhare I wont and do anythang that suits my faincy. These kids know how to take care of themselves, cause' we taught em' our own ways". That was her speech, albeit bolstered from a bottle of courage.

The Alabaster Boy

Unable to stomach any more, Uncle John and Bushia left for Northwest Indiana and with them, the only protection or defense I had ever known.

For the rest of that Christmas season, things seemed to settle down. The next evening, Scottie and Edmund were dancing to the *Tennessee Waltz*, a song that haunted me for years afterwards, because it represented them trying to make believe that they loved each other. A love they both wanted to work, but failed. It could never have worked, because both were alcoholics, full of guilt because of their latest crimes against each other and their children. Both of them suffered from manic-depressive psychosis symptoms. I never knew which of them was going to show up, day or night. While in my

fifties, I was diagnosed as having a bi-polar personality with a chemical imbalance in my brain, which I handle with prayer and a fine family doctor.

CHAPTER 3—THE ALABASTER BOY

Nothing changed after the *Christmas from hell* and I knew more hell was on its way when the *old man's* army truck roared into the dirt yard of our shack one Friday afternoon. Walking directly to the refrigerator and looking inside, he slammed the door and shouted, "who ate all the f____n' hot dogs?" Red-eyed from whiskey and enraged because someone ate without his permission, he bellowed, "Joey, get in her right now." I ran in to the kitchen and stood at attention, as I gave an answer. "I age 2 hot dogs every day, because you and Mama were gone." He said, "when I was your age

The Alabaster Boy

nobody ate at all until *my* old man came home. Even if it was 10 o'clock at night. I told you to eat chili and bread all week, but that wasn't' good enough for you, was it?" With butterflies in my stomach and trembling with fright, I gave the wrong answer by saying "no," which enraged him. "Shut your lousy pie hole and bring a beer and the razor strap out to the back yard." I did what he said: shut my pie-hole by saying nothing more, found a beer, but not the strap and walked into the backyard to find the *old man* waiting upon his lawn chair throne, which sat in the middle of acres of dirt.

"Oh, so you couldn't find the strap, huh? Well grab that board over there, bring it here and bend over right in front of me." The pain was so severe. In fact, I cannot recall it, because my brain has blocked it out of my memory. He had an old fashioned radio hooked through the kitchen window by an extension cord and was listening to a baseball game, as I stood still in the center of his drunken wrath. At 3 years old, I took the pain like a man: never crying or begging for mercy. I simply waited for the buzzing noise to come. It faded into a white light. Edmund chewed snuff and ordered me to bring him two cans. "Now eat and swallow all of it, then maybe next time you'll think twice about eating without my permission," he snarled. "Now go hit the sack," he added. I heard him say, "he'll never eat hot dogs again."

Scottie arrived later finding the *old man* passed out in the lawn chair amidst his empire of dirt, with empty beer cans and a half pint of whiskey his only company. She found *me* in my little army cot, with welts oozing blood and fluids that made my flour sack shorts and T-shirt stick to me. Moving quickly, she soaked me in a tub of warm water until my soiled clothes fell off, allowing her to dress my wounds. Projectile vomiting, diarrhea, fever and blurred vision were handled by simple country medicines, handed down from her mother. For several hours, I either lapsed into semi-consciousness or fell into a very deep sleep.

The Alabaster Boy

That evening, Scottie, outraged at the *old man* for his unrestrained temper, battled physically from the kitchen into the garage and for once, was almost winning because Edmund was still drunk. Queenie, our Collie, rushed in to protect Scottie, tearing into the *old man's* arm, sending him staggering into the bathroom in search of the first aid kit. By all accounts, Scottie had scored at T.K.O., at least in the sense that she would not be used again as a human punching bag. Separated from the clamor of battle, I hid by the outside door of the garage, taking in everything. Standing next to a large floor safe, Scottie asked me if I knew the combination. "Of course you don't, Joy. You can't read," she said. Later, she found it and when the time came, took the *old man's* money. Queenie was extremely protective of Mama and us. There were times when I, as a toddler, would make it out to the road and be suddenly snatched by my diaper and carried back to safety, where my faithful dog would run about, nudging me in one direction or another, like a sheep dog at work.

Joseph Anthony

The *old man*, incensed at Queenie's victory, thought up some cruel schemes for vengeance. One day he called her to come to the car for a ride, which she loved and would come running and leap through the passenger side window onto the seat. Not *that* day, for when she leapt for the window…it was shut. The jolt knocked her unconscious and almost broke her neck.

When he wanted her to mate, he tied a rope around her chest, under the joints of her front legs and hung her up in the garage, in a position where any male dog could quickly enter her. Edmund didn't even want her to have the simple courtship that even an animal should be afforded. Once he was sure she was pregnant, he planted a large piece of copper screen just under a layer of dirt, outside of his window, where he drank and waited for males to come around. Wetting the dirt that covered the screen and attaching an electric wire to it, he plugged it in every time a suitor came to call, shocking both the visiting male and Queenie. That is

The Alabaster Boy

how he resolved every problem. Planning violence was his only path of logic. Acting it out: his only pleasure.

Try to imagine that all of this took place during the only Christmas I remember. It lasted for days and nights. If *that* was the season to be jolly, what would the *rest* of the year bring? I thought the reason Jesus came into this world was to *FREE* all of us and that's why we celebrate Christmas: God and man were reconciled. Some people refuse to be reconciled to peace, preferring a life of misery.

For the next few days, Mama nursed me back to health with freshly dressed bandages, goat's milk from the mother of our kid goats and freshly cooked wheat, grown on our rented land. So you see, dad did do *some* good things by raising crops. Soon I was up and running around the house and playing on the land. The country doctor present at my birth was right: I had proven to be strong and wiry despite the efforts of others.

During those few carefree days, I spotted a nickel on the floor and immediately swallowed it, but mother

Joseph Anthony

saw me and asked why. "I'm going to keep it for a ticket on the Greyhound bus," I answered. "But darlin', where will you go and how will you get the nickel out of your insides," she asked, trying to introduce logic to my thinking. Logic, however; escapes your thinking, when ruled by fear. She fed me lots of bread, helping me to pass the nickel and washed it off, giving it to me as a reward for eating so much bread.

"Daddy's gone for another week. Would you like to take the Greyhound bus to National City? The Fiesta De La Luna is there," she said. "What's that," I asked? "Oh, Sugar, it's a wonderful place with animals and clowns and rides. Everywhere you look will be cotton candy, games and lots of fun," she promised. "First, I'll fix us a special sandwich and bring a mason jar of Molly's milk, how's that?" I nodded my head in approval. Molly was the mother goat of Midgette, Bridgette and Buttercup. She stomped Buttercup to death in the woodpile, because Buttercup didn't look like Molly. That's what we guessed, but who knows the

The Alabaster Boy

mind of a goat? My brother Johnny was also treated different because he looked more like Scottie than Edmund, Jr. and I. He felt it. He knew it and he naturally rebelled against the unjust wrath that fell upon him, just because he *looked* like someone who was *also* disliked because of her looks, actions and where she was born. Do *you* judge people because of their looks?

The only game I remember is one in which I won a goldfish, which I carried home that night on the bus, being cautious to spill no water. While at the festival, I saw a drunk woman riding the horses on the merry go round. She was laughing and rocking wildly from side to side…until she broke the horse and was thrown to the ground, unable to move and lying motionless. The ambulance came quickly and I heard one of the attendants say something about a broken back. "My baby-my baby. Where's my baby," she cried. I couldn't help but see a mirror image of mama.

Arriving home, we were welcomed by the goats, Queenie, the chickens and my pet goose. He was white, big and fat. We all relaxed for the rest of the week, while nervousness made us wonder about the old man. What new demons of terror would seize his mind with uncontrollable anger, then guilt, then sorrow, then back to anger, completing the cycle he wished to escape from.

The whiskey bottle, Scottie and Edmund were a volatile mixture that exploded every weekend without fail. Today young people can experience danger by "Virtual Reality'. As children, we had *reality;* often brutal with occasional moments of pleasure that made it seem bearable. When times were good, they were *very* good. My father took us many places and did simple things with us that created a much stronger bond between us, despite memories of his dark side. Besides, almost everyone has a dark side but if we don't know them intimately, we never see it.

Edmund I call dad, when I recall the good times. He took us to Encinada, Mexico, where we camped on the beach, climbed the rocky shore while gathering

The Alabaster Boy

crabs, which he dumped into a boiling caldron. Underneath the sands of the campfire, baked potatoes waited. He taught us to swim there too, by throwing us off of the cliff into the ocean, but was always ready to save us if we failed to swim.

San Diego Naval base was our picnic site one day. Dad bought a large, oval can of sardines and some rye bread. We all ate sandwiches, while we listened to his wonderful stories about being in the war. Those topics are exciting to three boys. He truly loved us, but was daily tormented by suspicions of an unfaithful wife, giving vent to rage, which is blind to whom it hurts. Often times *we* were hurt for *her.* One day the big troop transport truck came roaring into the gravel driveway. "Who wants to go up to the camp with me for a week," he asked? We all shouted, "I do…I do!" I must have had the hungriest look on my face, for he chose me, gently placing an army cap on my head. It was too big, but I loved it. Edmund Jr. and Johnny cried, "but I wanna' go, Dad." Gracious words fell from my father's lips, assuring them that next week and the following week, each of them would go. There was fleeting joy in his eyes that were cradled in tears.

Daddy was sober and full of life, excited at the prospect of spending the next 3 weeks with each of *his* sons. He was an extremely handsome man with a sparkling, genuine smile. The kind that melted my heart. Riding up to the mountain camp was wonderful, bouncing around in the biggest truck I had ever seen, let alone actually ridden in. Watching my father operate the gear shift made me feel like a man. A *little* man, but a man. We slept in the U.S. Army barracks and I did not wet the bed all week, had Rice Crispies for breakfast and on the day of our departure, daddy brought me a surprise. It was an old-fashioned squeeze box, which I joyfully played, as we rolled down the mountain, bouncing and laughing, with me trying to keep my over-sized army hat on. I loved my daddy so very much that week. My brothers' love for him also grew stronger as each of their mountain trips manifested. Each time

The Alabaster Boy

he fought with Scottie, he packed us into the car and we camped out in the open, upon the beaches of Mexico, catching our own dinner and sleeping under the stars.

About a month after the Feast of the Moon, (Fiesta De La Luna) Johnny and I were moved into the garage and furnished with World War II bunk beds made out of angle iron frames. Our new relationship with daddy, prompted him to move us beyond the battle zone of the *Friday night fights*. Edmund, Jr. was kept in the house. First born rights, I suppose, but a dubious honor, considering the danger.

Edmund's plans to shield us from the violence failed. One night, terrible shouting, cursing and banging erupted, followed by breaking glass and one of Scottie's melodramatic screams. Storming into the garage she said, "Joy, your goldfish is dead. We'll get another one, but right now I have to take daddy to the hospital." She was out of the driveway in a matter of seconds, screaming down the road in that old Mercury. Johnny and I ran to the kitchen sink to find it blood-soaked with a broken, quart beer bottle lying in the middle. My goldfish was impaled on one of the pieces of glass. One of Dad's veins must have been cut, because he stayed in the hospital several days. The next morning I was assigned clean-up duty. My job was to clean the old Mercury's front foot wells, which were covered with coagulated blood. I used a towel to grab large globs of gelatin-like blood. It made me vomit. Years later, I would do the same thing, in a different place, but the *old man* would not survive that one.

The neighbors must have known what was going on all along, because the next Thanksgiving, they saw us kids sitting on the front porch and brought us some turkey and cranberry sauce. We didn't eat it because that Thanksgiving was spent at Blackie's farm, eating chicken, stuffing and a million other things. I must have been about four, but my father's legacy of violence had already been passed on to me. My cousin Clarence and I were playing up in a Walnut tree and suddenly I slammed him in the head with a hammer I had pulled

The Alabaster Boy

from my pocket. He fell from the tree. I felt nothing. I had definitely taken possession of the Walnut tree. Clarence later became a preacher, just like Grandma.

Back at the ranch, or house, Johnny and I were confined to the garage. It's where we lived. One day, we found some bamboo poles and a cat wandered into our domain.

Quickly, we leapt from our bunk beds and raced to shut the door. He was our prey now. We slowly beat him until he collapsed on the far wall of the garage. One more whack with the cane pole and yellowish excrement squirted out of him. One last, gasping howl told us he was almost finished. We pounced on the helpless animal like jackals, mashing the life out of him with the butts of the cane poles. Don't even *try* to tell me a parent doesn't influence their children.

Soon we captured every neighborhood animal we could, brought him into the garage and tortured it to death, burying the bodies at night, somewhere among the 125 acres. It wasn't long before we learned that using the *old man's* .22 rifle was much more efficient. All we had to do was wait and watch for any living creature, then squeeze the trigger and watch them roll over in the dirt, dead or dying. Why? Because *we* were dead, *inside*, so why should anything *else* live? The seeds of violence had been planted in my heart and would grow to an uncontrollable force over the coming years, being dormant during good times and rising out of me like a monster during bad times. At an early age, I was killing for fun, when other children were having nursery rhymes read to them by their mamas and daddies. Today's fictitious characters like Harry Potter and Buffy the Vampire Slayer, would have been considered a joke compared to the inner darkness and cruelty that now resided in me.

One day, my father said, "go and kill your pet goose. I'm gonna' make some blood soup." Without hesitation, I walked directly to the back yard and punched him in the neck with a shovel, partially severing his head. He ran about wildly, but I quickly caught him,

The Alabaster Boy

ripped off his head and brought his body right back to the garage. That place we called the dungeon, because of all the blood-letting that had taken place there. Was there ever *human* blood spilled there? What do you think Edmund and Scottie did there? Fights draw blood.

"Well done," said the *old man*, as I held the goose upside down, squeezing every drop of blood into the bucket below, filling it almost full for the blood soup my father favored. We ate it and liked it like lion cubs tasting their first kill, never going back to mother's milk if blood was available.

One night when I was 5 years old, daddy took me for a ride: a real treat anytime, if you could be assured of returning alive. Within minutes human blood *would* spill.

Rainy nights are dangerous for driving and can be deadly if the driver is drunk. The *old man* was that night. The result? The windshield on my side exploded into a spider web pattern, after my head slammed into it. In those days an ambulance was the forerunner to our present day paramedics, but apparently the attendants were well trained and must have released my dad and me to the police. Then again, maybe they were not so well trained, because I don't remember a single thing except suddenly being in a police station. "Where's Mama," I wondered? Watching the police lead Edmund into a cell and slam the door made me very sad. "He didn't do it on purpose," I said aloud. "Joey," said dad, "I got drunk and the cops are going to keep me here for a while and..." Then we looked at each other through the bars of the jail, sobbing and thinking we might never see each other again. "C'mon, kid," a cop said. "You have to go to the orphanage. Know why? Cause' your mother can't be found and we just can't let you go on your own. Besides...you see this paper," he asked? I nodded yes. "It says *she* was in jail too, 5 times, for being drunk, like you father is now." Obviously, there was no trauma counseling back then. As that blunt statement penetrated my mind, the buzzing sound came again, followed by the white light in my head. There

The Alabaster Boy

were a lot of time lapses that night. A pattern of syncope had already developed. I blacked out again. This would happen to me many times in later life, when I was suddenly confronted with some thing or act too terrible to face.

The nuns helped me not to wet the bed during the nights, by taking me to the potty during the night. Being gentle to me also helped dispel worry and anxiety. I liked the food and clean bed. I don't remember how long my stay in the orphanage lasted.

Out of the orphanage and enrolled in school, the other children walked down the sidewalk and into school, passing me by as I sat on the curb, certain I would not be admitted, because I had no socks or shoes. It never bothered me until I saw the other kids' new school outfits. It never bothered me, as my brothers and I ran daily through the terrain of southern California, always ending up at a hill, where we watched the immigration cops chase the wetbacks. Finally, my two brothers happened upon me and tried to encourage me.

Joseph Anthony

"Look, Joey. We're in second and third grade. Don't you think you should go inside and find out what first grade is like?" Then they left so they would be on time, while I ran the mile or so back home and retreated to the safety of the desert hills I had roamed so often. Eventually, I did show up at school and Mrs. Brown: my teacher, allowed me to attend bare-footed. Her old eyes surely saw the humiliation.

During that first year, I learned two things: don't lie and don't' steal, because you'll pay dearly for it when your old man finds out. One day the teacher asked us to color a paper. Looking at mine, she marked an x on it. I stayed a few minutes after school to salvage my paper from the trash can. I had crumpled it into a ball, but dug it out, straightened it up and broke into the teacher's desk, stealing one of her gold stars and pasting it on my crinkled paper. As I left, I spotted a powder blue, model airplane that belonged to a neighborhood girl playmate. I took that too. When asked about the star and airplane. I lied. Not just to the old man, but also to Mama. This

The Alabaster Boy

time they agreed with each other. The only thing that would stop my lies and stealing was a beating. My job once again, was to get the strap. Scottie was very angry and I really got it that time. That night I retrieved the nickel I had swallowed two years before and left the house after they had fallen asleep. By morning, I was extremely tired, but had made it to a park in National City. A fair distance even by adult standards.

In need of sleep, I hid inside a deserted railroad station that had piles of coal in it to feed the bellies of occasional old time locomotives that were a sight to see. On a piece of railroad track that was off to the side of the main line, sat one of these noble iron horses, stilled by progress. Laying down on one of the coal piles, I looked up and noticed some cob webs and missing strips of boards that once shielded the old depot from the elements. Beams of sunlight filtered through them, making the coal dust sparkle like diamonds. Jumping up, I stuffed my hobo-type rag at the end of my shoulder stick, with all of the coal it would fit. Now I was rich!

Joseph Anthony

The nickel I had saved, paled in comparison to my *Nuevo riches* and so I feel asleep dreaming of all the hot dogs I could eat, without anyone to say "no".

Startled by the policeman's hand upon my shoulder, I quickly realized my escape was ended and I would be returned to my parents for *protective* custody. That's a laugh. Years later, I would run away from home again, unsuccessfully, but would keep running…from my past and myself, until a certain person would meet me face to face, forcing me to change in order to live a life that had meaning. One in which *my* children would *never* know sexual, physical or mental abuse. Not as long as I remained living with them.

Protective custody began the next day. Remember the cinder block patio my father had built? The old man and Scottie sat half naked in it, drinking and laughing with no clothes on top. *He* spoke first. "Joey, come over here and suck my nipples," he commanded. Extremely reluctant, I didn't budge an inch until he shouted out his orders again, very loudly and violently, then

The Alabaster Boy

changed his mind and pushed me over to Scottie, who locked her legs around me. "Now," he ordered in his most threatening tone of voice, *"Suck!* Suck both your mother's tits until they're all sucked out." I sucked like my life depended on it and until my mouth wouldn't work anymore. Why they did it I'll never know, but I suspect they were both aroused, because after I started running toward the wood pile, I turned to look and saw them groping and squirming around, unable to restrain themselves.

What happened was not comforting, as it would be to an infant. Confused and sickened, my mind was numbed. The only emotion I remember was the fear that I might be called back to perform another act of sex that might be worse than the first. Running from the wood pile into the house, then into the bathroom, I looked at myself in the mirror and beheld an ugly image of a 5 year old, turned into a statue. One that at first glance, was white, yet almost opaque, but more transparent. This, to me, was the purity and innocence I once had.

Joseph Anthony

What ruined it all were the sins, mottled and streaked with guilt, shame and emotional damage. I had become an *alabaster* boy. Strike three. As I grew older different types of inhumane treatment and escalated violence would erode the Alabaster boy's shell, releasing all of the anger inside upon society. My only hope was to take *the cure* I would later hear about.

As months went by Scottie snuck us off to Oregon under cover of darkness, taking all of the *old man's* money from the safe, while he slept off another drunk. The Alabaster was starting to crack already. While in Portland, my brothers and I ran wild at night and didn't return until dawn. I don't know where mama was during those days, but we were free to break into cars, breaking their windows, slashing their tires and stealing everything that wasn't nailed down. One night we ransacked a yard of school buses, slashing the seats and breaking all the windows. We even set fire to a couple with flares were found inside them. Edmund Jr. was 8 years old, Johnnie 7 and I was now 6. The anger

The Alabaster Boy

and violence we suffered from our parents was already in it's next generation and if *we* raised *our* children the same way, it would go on and on, just as it had for generations past.

Winter was now upon us and Scottie was out of money, prompting her to seek reconciliation with Edmund. In the San Diego bus station, we watched them kiss and make up, as we had so many times before, but this would be the last time. Later, whenever us siblings were caught fighting, we were always told to kiss and make up, which meant nothing to me, because Edmund and Scottie often did, only to return to fighting again. When older, I considered a kiss merely a tool to get sex. Edmund was clean, sober and had a new car, lending credibility to the homecoming. A few days later Scottie arrived home from work and we were all gone. Edmund's plan was brutal and swift. That evening we crossed into Arizona.

CHAPTER 4—JOURNEY TO THE PROMISED LAND

The move my father made seems cruel, but it was better than staying with Scottie, for eventually, one would have murdered the other or both would have died. He never got over the terrible longing for Scottie and never remarried, whereas; Scottie married three more times, bringing that total to five marriages that ended in divorce. He filed for divorce by proxy soon afterwards, but the marriage was over long before that, because she drew near to him with her words, but was far away with her heart He loved her with a sick, possessive jealousy.

The Alabaster Boy

The morning we left was really fateful, for it determined my fate and instantly threw me into a new classification of child: one from a broken home. It was also a morning of new hope for my father as he piled *his* three boys from *his* loins into the new car, bought for one reason: the trip back to East Chicago, Indiana. He was finally returning home, like the prodigal son. First, however; he stopped in San Diego to buy us each a set of new clothes and shoes, so we would be presentable upon arrival. Then he pointed the 1951 Hudson Hornet east and never looked back.

My little boy heart knew I would never see my biological mother again, yet felt nothing. You see, a boy turned into alabaster cannot feel.

The sleek, black machine my father drove roared through the desert night at between 90 and 100 miles per hour. My eyes were riveted upon the old time, circular speedometer with fluorescent green dials that glowed in the dark. Its needle always bouncing between those two speeds. It was so very dark in the desert's howling

Joseph Anthony

wilderness that I couldn't even remember the California home we had just left. Never a home in reality, it was simply a house built upon the sands of a weak and sick relationship. A house warmed by the West Coast sun during the day and frozen by the evil chills of torment at night, as it welcomed demons of jealous rage and homicidal feelings. Young children are not supposed to comprehend these weightier matters, but apparently, I did. Perhaps too much.

Driving beyond human endurance, Edmund pushed himself until he had to pull off of the road to pass out and plug up the whiskey bottle. His tortured mind was screaming for a peaceful future, while unable to escape the past: what he had with his wife. Unrequited love for Scottie would haunt him for the remainder of his days, because he wouldn't let go. He couldn't let go, or so he thought, but I learned that there were lots of nice girls interested in him before he joined the service. Still in his mid 30's and divorced, he would have made a good match for someone from his old neighborhood.

The Alabaster Boy

A child quickly senses his parent's feelings, as I did, wondering about the same things my father did. I wondered about the future, but how do you convince a child that his future, which he's never seen, will be better than the past he has lived? How could I ever see myself as a rose, when all I had ever known was the fear of my parents and the violence that stuck me like the thorns of the cactus plants I once played in? The kind that stick deep into your heart. In addition, someone has to remove the thorns before the wounded heart can mend.

Winter winds that sweep down from Canada across the Great Lakes are so cold it actually feels like they're burning. We met them head on as they skipped around the southern curve of Lake Michigan into Northwest Indiana: our destination. Heavy, wet snow and ice quickly piled up on the windshield wipers, forcing them into hard labor with heavy a click-clack rhythm that barely kept the windshield clean.

Joseph Anthony

When I awoke in the back seat my first question was where we were, because I had never seen snow nor felt cold before. My father said, "before I answer all of your questions, I just want you to know why I left your mother. It's because she did some bad things. Things you wouldn't understand now, but will when you're older. I love her but I hate her for what she did to me and you kids." Father was hurt and crying and wiping his eyes with his shirt sleeve so he could see. Like any child, I didn't want to see either mother or father hurt. Children don't want grief or sorrow.

"I hate her too," I blurted out. That's when daddy switched personalities and changed back into the *old man*, screaming, "don't you *EVER* say that about your mother again!" Feeling nothing I simply said, "okay, but where are we?" His tears abated and in a few minutes he answered, "in Kankakee, Illinois, but it won't be long now. Are your new pants wet? If they are we'll have to figure out some way to dry them." I lied to him. "No… they're dry," I said, remembering the special Christmas

The Alabaster Boy

gifts I received for wetting the bed. Curling up in the back seat again, I escaped from fear and drifted into the protective world of slumber: a habit that accompanied me for years. Whenever pressure was brought to bear upon me…pressure that seemed too great to handle, I used sleep as an escape mechanism.

The powerful new sedan screamed defiantly at the Midwest winter, ripping it's way into the promised land of East Chicago. For a very short time the Kankakee River was to us, what the River Jordan was to the Hebrew children of Egypt: the last obstacle to surmount before reaching a place that flowed with milk and honey. Father surmounted the river's bridge with a reckless, blistering speed that made the old, steel bridge rumble, leaving a cloud of swirling snow behind. He loved to drive fast, drink hard, thrill women and fish his limit.

The thing he loved most was a real, knockdown, drag out fight where the winner takes all. He always fought to the death and always won. I was with him, in Dyer, Indiana, when at the age of 54, he took on six men in their early twenties and faced them all down, one by one, by pointing a pistol at each of their heads, asking them if they wanted to die. Of course, by that time, he had become a legend in his own mind, praying for someone to try something, while other men his age were just being introduced to their latest offspring, as…grandpa. He *also* was given four grandchildren by us three boys and for a while, it seemed like he had a reason to live when he was around them, although calling my own childhood made me watch him like a hawk.

The sound of our whining tires upon the steel deck of the bridge awakened me in time to see the old, green structure become a thing of the past…like California had, disappearing through the back window.

Draping myself over the front seat, so I wouldn't miss one word, I questioned my father. "Where are we now," I asked? "About sixty miles from East Chicago," he answered. "What's East Chicago," I asked? "Its

The Alabaster Boy

home for you now…or will be. I grew up there. Now *you'll* grow up there and have the kind of life I've always wanted for you. No more whippings, fights, drinking and no more running down to Blackie's bar to warn your mother. Her name will not be spoken in our new place," he said.

Sober for the first time since we left California, I believed him. I was officially free of the woman known as my mother and should never let her name pass over my lips again. "What if someone freed me from my father too," I thought? "I would be alone.

Oh well, if that happened, I could always find my way back to the railroad depot in National City, California. I could hop a freight train to get there and *next* time no railroad dick would find me.

An hour or so passed, when suddenly daddy let out a wail like that of a wild man exclaiming, "wake up kids, we're at the corner of Indianapolis Boulevard and 151st street. Look! There's Chuck and Irene's tavern… still in business. Wish I could stop for a couple of

Joseph Anthony

brews, but Bushia and Aunt Celia would probably say something about it." We were only about six blocks from Bushia's (grandma) house when he ordered, "straighten your clothes and put your shoes on, otherwise; they'll think you're a bunch of wild Indians, when in fact, we had always been that way. Running wild through the hills and fields of cactus and peppers barefoot allowed the sun to bake us as dark as the wetbacks we watched cross over the border everyday.

It was October 31st and as we stood on Bushia's porch, in new clothes that covered our filth, the door opened and a woman with an inviting smile welcomed us, but I wouldn't go, so she patiently coaxed me over the threshold. Then she gently put her arms around me and carried me into the warm light of the home. It was my dad's sister: aunt Celia.

She immediately sensed the nervousness and reluctance in me, as I moved stiffly, uncertain of this new environment. "Eddie," she asked, what has happened to these kids? They look like they've never seen a bath and

The Alabaster Boy

this baby's afraid of everything. His arms are wrapped so tight around me I can barely breathe." Edmund's answer to her was, "bull shit. Joey's never been afraid of anything." She countered by asking, "then why is he acting like a dog that's been beaten?" There was no answer, but Bushia was taking it all in, not fooled by the new clothes, for she remembered her trip to California with my Uncle John. Memories of such sever child abuse are not soon forgotten by a child's grandmother. Edmund was her first son by her first husband and it hurt her old heart to know he had mistreated her grandchildren.

"Well," said Aunt Celia, "let's see if a little boy like you would like some homemade hot bread and butter." Placing it before me, I just stood there, afraid to touch it for fear of being beaten, so I just looked down at the floor. In California I was punished for the crime of eating. Did people here do the same? Finally convinced that it was okay to eat, I enjoyed my first taste of Bushia's home-baked bread with real butter.

Joseph Anthony

Exhausted from the long trip, my mind could scarcely believe my Aunt Celia picking me up, placing me in a bathtub and feeding me. My fondest memories are of being carried in her arms, because I felt wanted and loved. Unprepared for my sudden arrival, she wrapped me in a large flannel shirt, which served as a nightgown. The kind little boys wore years ago. Then she carried me into Bushia's bedroom and tucked me in under warm blankets, sealing my emotions and settling my heart with a warm kiss only a *real* mother could give. I feel asleep and dreamed about this warm woman with the beautiful smile, who showed me more love in one night, than I had experienced during my entire, short life.

It seemed like a very short time before Bushia awoke, yelling something in Polish. I had wet her bed and had to change into something dry. Passing through the living room and rubbing my eyes, I saw Elaine and Tommy for the first time. They were Aunt Celia's real children. Maybe if I tried real hard, I too could

The Alabaster Boy

be one of her children. Although Elaine didn't know it, I looked deep into her eyes and saw the same love and warmth that Aunt Celia showed me. A child sees things very clearly and simply, because their minds are not burdened with the cares of the world. At least they shouldn't be.

Elaine softly laughed at the sight she beheld, but she was laughing *with* me...out of joy, not *at* me, out of mockery. That night, after new dry clothes were given me, I fell asleep again. This time for the entire night and dreamed again of the tender woman called Aunt Celia, but also of my new-found cousin, who laughed softly. I dreamed of Elaine, not knowing that in the future, I would try too hard to please her, only to have things backfire, disappointing her. For now though, all I had to do was keep the bed dry. What amazed me was that even when I wet the bed, I was not beaten.

As I grew older, I was enamored with Elaine and fell in love with her, although she didn't know. I suppose it was only natural to feel romantic towards someone who lavished me with affection, personally groomed me and encouraged me as a young man. She was always gracious and waiting to receive me: the black sheep, with open arms. I shall always love Elaine Oakley, simply for who she is, not only for what she did for me. My father bought me some cheap and ugly attire for my eighth grade graduation. Clothes that a homeless person would turn down. When she saw them, she said, "this will never do" and with her own money, bought me a brand new, very fashionable suit with all of the matching accessories. That is another thing I shall never forget. She is gorgeous. The most lovely, feminine woman I have ever met. She has a smile that could melt the coldest heart. A radiant, golden skin, soft and full lips give her a sensual look most movie stars would give anything for. She is beautiful. The epitome of womanhood and married to the most blessed guy in the world, who is the epitome of manhood. John Oakley is his name. He too, was and is the ideal father and husband. No one could ask for more. He was a success in the

The Alabaster Boy

business world, just as he was as head of his household. Together they have raised four fine sons, attending all of their children's activities and gladly providing the love and care so necessary to every child. Elaine has spent her entire life working, loving and helping those in need, both as a nurse and in her private life. Today she still finds time for others. Why? Because she is full of love. Elaine has always had natural elegance, lovely manners and an honest, graceful way about her. If you visit her home you will leave thinking you have just been in the company of a queen; indeed, she wears her invisible crown with ease and dignity, never regarding herself as better than others. Oh, how I wish every child could have such a family. At the time of this writing, John and Elaine Oakley have been married forty-five years. That is a testimony to enduring love and family values that most other American parents desperately need to learn. They deserve to be called the standard bearers of all that a couple and family can be.

CHAPTER 5—A ROSE GREW AMONG THE LILACS

All of the nurturing treatment I received during those first few days at Bushia's house could be compared to the *urgent* care one is given at today's clinics. While addressing my immediate needs, Aunt Celia and Elaine knew some long term treatment was required to cure the cause. Treating the *symptoms;* however; began the next night, when I discovered Aunt Celia had raised the standard of child-bathing from a mere bath into an art form. First came the lengthy soaking, then scrubbing. Afterwards, I stood up in the tub, covered with bubbles while she emptied the dirty water, rinsed me and refilled the tub. This process was repeated three times and each time I heard, "there is so much dirt in your ears, you could grow potatoes in them." More than wonderful, more than delightful, it was an event…for *both* of us. She cleansed me from the crown of my head to the soles of my feet and did it on her knees at the side of the bathtub. Her back must have ached and I'm sure she was tired, but she never complained, giving up her evening for my benefit.

When the last drop of rinse water trickled down the drain, she wrapped me in a large, soft towel and brushed my hair for the first time. The fragrance from my *new* mama's soap was so refreshing and sweet…I just stood there and enjoyed it, breathing in a renewed sense of worth, comfort and most of all…belonging some *place* and to some *one.*

The towel slipped from my little body without my noticing, because I was warm all over with the feeling of comfort that had never been mine before.

"Joey, aren't you going to dry yourself," she asked? "You'll catch a chill if you don't", she added..

I did not know *how* to dry myself. How *could* I if I never bathed myself? Sensing all of that, she dried me with so much motherly gentleness and love, I felt certain that Jesus Himself had blown a warm breath over me.

She also probably sensed that I could not dress myself either. After all, the only practice I had was when my father dressed me in the new clothes he had bought for the trip from California. Clothes we wore for the entire trip, never undressing, because we slept in the car.

"Joey. Open your arms and close your eyes, 'cause I'm going to give you a nice surprise," she said. "Okay…you can open your eyes now." When I opened my eyes I saw her kneeling right in front of me, holding a pair of flannel pajamas that were decorated with cowboys, Indians, and covered wagons. In addition, she handed me my first pair of 'big boy' underwear.

The Alabaster Boy

"These are special because they're just for you. Do you like them," she asked? Speechless, my eyes welled up with tears of thanksgiving, as I tried to slip into my new big boy shorts, but put them on backwards. She smiled and laughed softly, but as she dressed me, I saw *her* eyes water. She was filled with the hurt that only a *real* mother could feel, as my newly cleansed body revealed lumps and bruises and a few scars that no child could self inflict. She had raised a girl and boy, but had never beaten them like an animal, or forced them to perform sexual acts. I could see her eyes questioned where all the marks came from, but was wise enough not to ask, knowing I'd remain silent. "Well," she sniffled, "let's see how well they fit and then, we'll have a special, bedtime treat: Ovaltine and hot buttered bread." My only response was, "gee, Aunt Celia, now I smell just like a rose." It wasn't until years later that I learned she had carried that phrase deep within for her entire life.

Soon she rented the basement apartment of her home to my father and life took on a new meaning.

Joseph Anthony

Aunt Celia and her husband: Uncle Stanley had a small Ma and Pa store, complete with a butcher shop, next door to the house. Enjoying her company, I spent all the time I could in that store, watching her and learning from her dealings with the neighborhood patrons. Of course, there were many poor souls around and each who wandered in left with a couple of home made, fresh sandwiches and a quart of milk. "There's always room for kindness," she said, "besides, there but for the grace of God, go I." My child's approach to God understood.

Because Uncle Stanley worked different shifts at the refinery, he could not always be there to help Aunt Celia at close of business, but when he could, early evenings found her next door, at her upstairs home, making dinner and caring for *her* family. I shall always remember the sounds of a peaceful family, discussing topics at the dinner table punctuated with laughter and the joyful sounds of rattling pots and pans. I always wondered what types of nice meals were being fixed. Wanting desperately to be a part of it all, I climbed

The Alabaster Boy

the stairs half way many times, but knowing I didn't belong, returned to our garden apartment. My brothers wondered what was bothering me, but I remained aloof, suppressing all emotion.

Downstairs, I watched daily for my father's return from work, making sure I had freshly brewed coffee ready for his arrival. If he walked in and didn't literally see the coffee perking, he immediately turned the burner on again, breathed deeply and loudly, angry and likely to lash out at me for such an infraction. Soon I resolved the great percolator problem by brewing the coffee until done, watching for his footsteps and rushing to turn the burner on again. Within seconds, it was bubbling, leaving no question that it was scalding and strong. In time, the *BOYS*, as we were called, always had a hot meal prepared for him, just so he could have something nice after a hard day at the Portland Cement Company. One very positive result of our culinary efforts was that we all became self-sufficient at an early

Joseph Anthony

age and I, quite the gourmet by the time I reached my early twenties.

Everything went fine for a short time. The old California life was forgotten, as I embraced the new world of the Midwest, with its snowflakes, steel mills and rich traditions of family and hard work ethics. The greatest blessings, however; were no more drinking and violence, although short-lived and two women who loved me for the child I was. Life began to have purpose and my love for Aunt Celia and Elaine grew very strong, yet very quietly, lest my father find out that I felt warm when in *their* company, while terrified of each moment spent in *his* presence and that of his black razor strap, which he used as a scepter, to rule his subjects.

Saint Peter said, "a dog always returns to his own vomit." So it was with my father, I soon found. Every day at precisely 4:30 p.m., I waited to see if dad or the *Old man* would show up after work. If he had stopped at any of the local taverns, it would be far into the night before he darkened our doorway. No need to keep a

The Alabaster Boy

vigilant watch over the coffee in that case. The alarms within me went off loud and clear one day because the *old man* came home that night, acting strange, just like he did back in the old days of California. He was drunk and the honeymoon was over. Violence would soon become a nightly visitor to our once-peaceful garden apartment.

Aunt Celia had no way of knowing if beatings or blessings were being administered unless she heard his booming voice threatening to kill us, because we had failed in some way or another. Most of the time he would grit his teeth and pound his fists on the supper table, saying, "one of these days I'm going to murder you with my bare hands!" Neither could Aunt Celia know if his frayed nerves, caused by drinking, would give way to an emotional breakdown. His rage paralyzed us boys with fear…unable to speak or move. Just like a deer caught in the headlights.

When he was sober, he was naturally mean, a man of few words and cheap, always resorting to violence in order to impose his will. When drinking, he gave a new meaning to the word 'cruelty'. He began to go on three week benders, embarrassing us when his foreman came to our door before his shift, demanding to see this man so sick that his children had to call-in the excuse from a pay phone. If only the foreman would have known how really sick the *old man* was.

During those times, vulgar language and beatings spewed forth and the razor strap was resurrected. Sometimes we boys were whipped because we simply didn't understand the written directions he left when he went to work. One night I stayed up until midnight, scrubbing the entire bathroom with…yes, a toothbrush. "Good", he said, "now go to bed and I'll be in to give you a kiss in a little while". Surprisingly, he did, but he smelled awful and that odor, coupled with the not too distant memories of California, made me sick. Waiting until he passed out, I went into the bathroom, vomited and spent the night in a series of nightmares: those which had been and those which I feared would come.

The Alabaster Boy

Aunt Celia was upstairs when the old man ripped into his infamous speech. The one I feel broke him and her apart forever. It almost tore me apart. For a number of years, I became wayward, being void of all emotions and desperate for guidance. We actually never knew whether we were doing right or wrong…in his mind. Anything we did might incur his wrath and the tragedy was that we didn't know why.

The state of our union address began by Edmund, Sr. ordering Edmund, Jr. to go get the strap, even though we did nothing wrong. I will not even attempt to describe the horror we three boys endured that night, except to say that by the time Aunt Celia had burst through the door, we were all swollen, red and crying. I did not want to cry, because I thought Aunt Celia would think her little *rose* had done something wrong. My little heart couldn't bear that. I loved her.

"Eddie," why call these children such awful names," she asked? "I can hear it all the way upstairs. Why the beatings every day? These boys have never known a real mother and I think I've done a pretty good job. What's wrong…what's bothering you? Do you want to go back to Scottie? Do you want Scottie to come here? Well, make up your mind. If you want to get back together with her, at least leave the kids, so they'll have a chance with a *REAL* mother," she demanded. The *old man* made a third choice. "We'll move out. Now get out of here," he said using expletives freely.

Making good his threat, we moved to another apartment within several years, with my father always asking us if we had seen or talked to Aunt Celia. He had torn me away from Aunt Celia and Elaine: the only two women I ever loved; my connection with them growing slighter, as did theirs and it was neither of our choices.

Let us take an excursion into the good times… before the break up. Coming home one day at lunch, Aunt Celia made me a fresh, sausage sandwich with mustard and onions. Food isn't everything, but at my present age of 57, I still prefer that sandwich.

The Alabaster Boy

While in third grade, I misbehaved and sister Collette over reacted with the beating stick she carried. When I came home, Aunt Celia, whom I now considered my mama, saw me scratching at the wounds, which were trying to heal. "What's wrong Joey," she asked? When the whole story came out, she walked me to school the following morning and spoke to the nun. *No* one damages this little boy again. With all of your education, can't you see he's been damaged enough? What could this child possibly have done that was so bad a beating was required"? When I went to sleep that night, my bedtime prayers included a special thanksgiving and a special request: "thank you, Lord for my *new* mama and please make her love me always as her own, youngest baby." God *did* answer that prayer in time, bringing us so much closer, that today it seems strange if we don't affectionately called each other *mom* and *son*. Her son and daughter call her mother, but to me she will always be *mama.*

Joseph Anthony

Other cherished memories were born in mama's garden apartment. The kind that served to balance my life, at least to some degree. There was a special, family, dinner every Christmas eve, prepared in the old world tradition. Included were courses of kraut, baked fish, borsch, sausage and many other original recipes. Best of all was when the wafer was passed from one family member to another, wishing every good thing upon everyone. Similar to Passover, but of Polish-Catholic origin. The Christmas tree was decorated simply but beautifully and there was a certain reverence for it. We children were not allowed to assail it in one mad rush to get our little hands on everything that existed. Instead, a gift was really a present, handed gently to someone, with love and a kind wish…while we were all still gathered at the table of fellowship.

There was ice skating too. Not skating at the park in a meaningless circle, but running off to the nearby canal, wearing a black cape like Zorro, fashioned from a black slip of mama's. She's never known it, but now

The Alabaster Boy

that I've kept it a secret for around 40 years, I think she'll be able to laugh about it.

First tie the cape around your neck, then feel it fly in the wintry wind, as you race hundreds of yards down the Little Calumet River, dodging debris frozen in the ice. Yeh! Now that's ice skating. It was exciting and dangerous. An actual obstacle course in the dark, caused by factories dumping their waste wherever they pleased. The big trick was knowing where the soft spots were. I found one on a night when none of the other boys showed up…but Martin did and pulled me from the blackness of the icy water below and carried me to his fire under the bridge, wrapping me in an old blanket. That's where he lived and that's where **I** lived, not died that night. Had it not been for him, then mama Elaine and possibly even the *old man* would have gathered to mourn me as my body lay in a small, child's casket. I'm *certain* Martin would have come.

Arriving home, I looked like I did on any other ice skating night, having been cunning enough to roll around in the snow before I made my entrance, explaining my wet clothes.

Mama's store always had homemade, Polish sausage. Whenever it was made, my brothers and I carried it to a nearby, brick smoking house, waited inside all day until it was done, then lugged it home on a long pole, always sampling some.

Other ma and pa stores made sausage too, so I got a hold of several links from them, rather than cut into mom's profit. That evening I took a dime to Golan's bakery, bought a loaf of hot Vienna rye bread and paid Martin a visit under the bridge.

We soon became friends and during his daylight walks through the neighborhood, he would stop for me and we would talk of many things. When night fell, I would often visit his humble home beneath the bridge. Now maybe you can see that a trip to the park just couldn't compare to a rendezvous on the river. Other kids were afraid of Martin, but little Joey feared nothing…except being unloved.

The Alabaster Boy

When Spring gave way to Summer, mama found good and useful chores to occupy our time: trimming the grass, stacking cases and boxes on the store shelves and learning to use the big, stainless steel, meat slicer and meat grinder. We made sausage, hamburger and all of the items a good butcher shop should have. I must admit, she had a very good mind for business. My favorite chore, however; was tending her garden in the middle of the back yard. Filled with a variety of flowers, plants and shrubs, my favorite was the Lilac bush.

Every Mother's Day, I would pick a handful and tie them to a cheap bottle of perfume with a piece of ribbon I had purchased from the five and dime store. With each annual effort, I was rewarded with a soft kiss and heard a loving "thank you Joey." Then she would draw me into her bosom and wrap her arms around me, holding me for a few seconds. She knew she was the only mother I had.

It wasn't too long before I was allowed to come upstairs to help her wash and dry dishes. Oh, I broke a few at first, but she never said a word. Soon I was underfoot almost all the time. One morning, I stood watching her standing in front of the bathroom mirror, putting on make-up. She noticed me and my tears and asked, "what's the matter, Joey?" Unable to hold it inside any longer, after all she had become to me, I uttered these few words: "I love you. do you think you could ever become my mother?" I'm sure she was stunned. Tommy and Elaine were already graduating college and would soon be married and I'm sure she was looking forward to grandchildren. She answered in this manner: "I'll have to ask Uncle Stanley first, because if I'm going to be your mother…he will have to be your father, because we're married. Do you want me to ask him?" After a long silence I spoke. "I…I…I just don't want to have to say happy Mother's Day *Aunt Celia* anymore. I want to say…"then I shut up. **"*What* do you want to say, Joey"? Then I blurted it out. "I want to be able to call you *mama* on Mother's Day. That isn't all, either. I'll bring you a bottle of *Bubble-Up* every night and rub your feet

The Alabaster Boy

and won't break any more dishes and I'll be nice when I take Penny (her dog) out. I'll be quiet when you watch the Ed Sullivan show and Lawrence Walk. I'll be very good." Then she said, "come here, Joey" and held me. I could feel her shake and her stomach heave against me. As she wept silently, I understood she could never be my mother in name, even though she had been in deed for such a long time. "Anytime you want to come upstairs and rub my feet after a hard day at the store… well, these old dogs could use it," she laughingly said. "And anytime you feel lonely, especially on Sundays, you just come right up here and we'll keep each other company and watch TV."

Slowly, over the next year, I became a permanent fixture upstairs and being around all the time created many opportunities for trouble that a little boy easily falls into. There was punishment when I was bad, but not homicidal attacks. There were also rewards, when I was good, but not overindulgence that would spoil me. Many of my tears found her apron, through joy and sorrow. Some of her tears found me and I gladly soaked them up deep into my soul, like a sponge crying out for the moisture of emotion.

Lessons were learned at her knee that have carried me though hell and back, always victoriously. Blessed memories were carried away from her upstairs home I occasionally shared. Memories that cannot be destroyed. Even though torn asunder from her by my father's jealousy (that I would love *her* more that his Scottie) the wound in my heart healed. It took years, but it healed. Love still lives in me.

We see each other again now, whenever possible and write and call on a frequent basis. More often than not, when we do, she likes to remind me of the bath she gave me, as a baby, when I said, "Aunt Celia, now I smell just like a rose."

That one act of motherly and unselfish love planted and nurtured a seed within me that became a rose during childhood, when I played in the yard, by the flower bed she loved so much. Hundreds of her other kind moments has transformed me into a rose that grew among the lilacs. Not a normal rose either, that eventually dies on the vine. To the contrary, *this* rose continues to blossom, returning the love that was given. Not only to mom, but each person I meet. Who knows if long ago they too were a California cactus? Who knows if they suffered as I did and they too are searching for a haven of rest?

CHAPTER 6—OUT OF CONTROL

Before moving from mama's downstairs apartment, the old man's drinking reached the point of Delirium Tantrums, commonly called the D.T.'s. Each morning he screamed with fright for hours, begging snakes, devils, spiders, and mad dogs with horns to leave him alone, but they would not, so a decision was made to commit him to a psychiatric ward for acute alcoholism. Electrical shock treatments easily turn a strong-willed man into a mindless robot. There were no charter hospitals or Betty Ford clinics then and a patient was not released until a shrink signed the papers, which

The Alabaster Boy

left my brothers and I free to wreak havoc for a long time.

Each evening I snuck out and raided caboose cars on the tracks that ran through the magnesium factory, gathering flares, pieces of magnesium, railroad torpedoes and every other type of explosive available… for future uses. Sneaking out was easier than sneaking back in undetected by Uncle Stanley, who was doing his best to double as a temporary father, while the old man was getting his brain fried daily at the nut house. While attempting to climb through the basement window, Uncle Stanley surprised me one midnight. The new blue and gray winter coat had a large hole burned through the pocket, where I had hidden a smoldering railroad flare in a desperate escape from one of the railroad dicks. I begged him not to tell Aunt Celia, who was in the same hospital as the old man, being treated for stress and nervous disorders. The coat was a gift from her. He said "okay" if I promised to be good, but my new resolve soon crumbled under temptation. Each night I stared out the window with my older brothers, discussing how fast the old man's new Pontiac was. Edmund Jr., 14, had extra keys made and for two weeks, every night, we went on wild adventures, drag racing, joy riding and frequenting the local drive-in restaurants, trying to impress the waitresses who roller skated up to the driver's window and talked mainly to Edmund and Johnny. I was 12 years old so my place was in the back seat, until it was my turn to drive, mostly on a dark country road where chances of a wreck were least. How are *your* children going to learn to drive? Many times we exceeded 115 mph. We were caught at that game too and when the old man came home from the hospital, Edmund was sent to a seminary and Johnny and I to another school, about 8 blocks away.

The old man figured the notorious Father Rocco would straighten us out. He was wrong. A new apartment and school was not the answer.

No longer a student at St. Stanislaus, I easily made friends at Immaculate Conception, where the

The Alabaster Boy

boys were much rougher at a younger age. It was predominately an Italian, Roman Catholic school, with a fierce rivalry existing between both. So fierce, in fact, that frequent gang wars broke out. After one very brutal confrontation, Father Rocco gathered all the boys in 7th and 8th grade and herded us into the church. With a whipping stick in one hand and a smoking cigar in the corner of his mouth, he delivered a blistering speech, backed up by blistering actions and soon the local police captain proclaimed the neighborhood safe again.

Milder boyhood pranks replaced rumbles for a short time. Several blocks from the church was a four story building that was an apartment building and whore house with the bottom level being a bar. The front door was built on the corner, so the bartender could easily notify tenants of any police who came calling, which was usually for the 'Friday night fights'. We called it the Bee Hive because it was always buzzing with activities of the wrong kind. Being too young to go inside, my new Italian buddies and I would sit caddy-corner on

Joseph Anthony

Friday nights and watch drunken men and women fight. Sometimes they tumbled out the door and other times flew out the window, spewing broken glass and curse words until the cops came. The real name of the place was Topsie's and was the closest thing I have ever experienced to an old west saloon. After the police left was the safest time for the weekly shipment of Alabama moonshine to be delivered. That's where *we* came in. Being young, small and quick, a small band of us could carry a small truckload (about 50 cases) up to the fourth story backroom within 25 minutes, earning $.75 a case. That's almost $10 dollars for each kid for a half hour of work. In addition, we usually received a mason jar of White Lighting to split among four boys. There was no detectable smell on our breath, because it was mainly grain alcohol made from corn squeezins'.

Henry the driver, spent each Friday night in one of the flop house rooms, after sampling his cargo, then, passed out, dead to the world. On one such evening, we snuck into Henry's room, unzipped his pants and painted

The Alabaster Boy

his penis black with shoe polish, being sure to arrive at the hallway bathroom, near his room, early Saturday morning. His screams of unbelief echoed throughout Topsie's, as he relieved himself and we ran away down the hallway, laughing all the way. These types of pranks soon became boring, forcing me to find other avenues of excitement and earn more money through more dangerous enterprises. There *were* certain people who offered just such opportunities, I discovered.

Entering high school in 1960 brought new problems, mostly in the form of gangs of juniors and seniors who robbed and beat me and my brother daily. There was Jimmy: head of the polish gang. Joe and Tim Gaiterno: chiefs of the Italian gang and state champion wrestlers of the school, as well as bosses of Tony's pool room, our favorite hang out. Additionally there was Maurice and his black gang and the Puerto Rican and Mexican gangs, who only rode through the north Italian neighborhood, looking for a loner. In short, we had to pass through 5 gauntlets every day in order to make it to school.

Summer break came and with it, the realization that *something* had to be done to avoid another year of beatings and rubbings. For some reason, I realized at a very young age, my gift of lying and manipulating. That summer, I used it. First I set up the Puerto Ricans against the Mexicans with a few phone calls. Within days, the Puerto Ricans lost their foothold. Another phone call to the Mexican gang, advised them that there would be several white boys walking alone down the street from the pool room about 11:00 p.m.: a target they couldn't resist. Then I ran to the pool room and did one of my best acting jobs ever, shouting to the Gaiterno brothers "carloads of Mexicans from the harbor are on their way with guns. They're gonna' shoot us." Within minutes, the brothers had allies waiting in every alley with clubs while Tony's pool room was locked and dark. The Mexicans rolled down Olcott street slowly, looking hard for the white boys who were supposed

The Alabaster Boy

to be walking down the street. Coming to a dead end, they pulled into an alley to turn around and the local boys opened up on them. The Mexicans limped out of town, but still, Jimmy and his polish gang were left sharing power with the Gaiterno brothers. It was already August. School would soon begin and there was the gnawing problem of Maurice and his Black Cobra gang. What was I to do, short of quitting school? If I did that, there was the old man to reckon with. That would be worse than any 18 year old.

Quite by accident the answer came, when one afternoon, I walked up to the pool room and found my brother, Johnny bleeding from his head. Jimmy had done it. Enraged I hollered out loud, "Yimmeck (Polish for Jimmy)…come outside." Jimmy and his gang all laughed at a 14 year old threatening a six-foot, 18 year old. Finally, after calling him names, he came out, grabbed me and dragged me into the alley, where no one could see, but everyone, including a few of my *own* little gang, gathered round to watch the slaughter. He had me in a headlock and used my head as a battering ram against the brick wall. Within minutes, I was covered with blood that was covered with cinders and dust, but I held on like a bull-dog. He said, "you're pretty tough, kid. Do you give up?" I shouted "no." Then he made a serious mistake: he let me go. While my head was being scraped against the brick wall, I wiped the blood from my eyes with my shirt and saw a car battery laying there. When Jimmy let me go, he dropped to his hands and knees to rest. Right then I grabbed the battery and threw it, breaking his arm.

All my gang began to shout "Joe don't play," as his buddies took him away. Tony: the owner said, "bravo, Guiseppe, bravo." It was over. Jimmy never bothered me again and lost *his* hold on Tony's pool room too. Now only the Gaiternos and Maurice were threats.

The 1st of September arrived with the Gaiterno brothers firmly in control. What Joe and Tim Gaiterno controlled was not simply a pool room, but the flow of money, which they had to report to older men. It was a very serious responsibility and failure or skimming always proved to be fatal. The money came from illegal activities and Tony's pool room was the center of all operations in Little Italy's north sector.

Ace, just out of the Navy, walked into the pool hall one night. He had been 'All Navy welterweight and middleweight boxing champion' for 3 years straight. He quickly became friends and an ally with the younger boys like me. Joe and Tim Gaiterno entered the pool hall one night, while Ace and I were shooting a game of 8-ball. "Get off my table and give me half the table fee," said the younger Tim to Ace. Without a word, Ace shot out a left jab, stunning Tim. The older Gaiterno rushed Ace and was just as easily dispatched. They rant out of the pool hall with their tails tucked between their legs, as Tony shouted "bravo, Ace, bravo." He would always shout that to whoever was the latest victor. That night, he proclaimed Ace as the new king of operations. That left Maurice, who became suddenly respectful once my brother Johnny started carrying a .38 to school. My sophomore year was free of beatings.

Returning to roaming the streets and alleys of the industrial area at nights, I built a hidden fort, which serviced as an execution site for any dog or cat I captured. That was my way of striking back at my own abusers, who were bigger than me, leaving me helpless. Each time I killed an animal, I saw myself being killed. In a strange way, I was controlling my life or death. When the dog or cat was dead, I took the body to any garage I could find and set everything on fire. In my mind, the innocent dog or cat must have been guilty, in order to deserve such torture and death, so my last act was to cast them into the eternal fires. After all, they must have sinned when they were puppies and kittens, just as I must have sinned as a baby.

One night I captured a half grown puppy, brought him to the execution site and hung him, but only until he lost control of his bowels. Then I let him down to regain

The Alabaster Boy

consciousness, only to hang him again and again. I let him go after the fourth hanging.

My old man told me he used to destroy unwanted neighborhood cats for 25 cents a piece. I did it for nothing but meanness, throwing them into the same canal my father did years ago. Snatching a kitten from the railroad yards, I quickly dumped him into a gunny sack, securing him until I was ready to release him near the edge of the canal. It would be his final release…from torment, torture, abuse and he would find rest from an undeserved journey. Throwing him into the canal, I was surprised to see him overcome the current and pulled him from the bank, letting him rest…until he scratched me. The next time I flung him as far out into the canal as I could. After a while, he began to lose strength. I stood watching him look into my eyes as his only salvation, until drowning.

Before too long, I found the ultimate killing field: a slaughter market: a place where I could kill larger animals with much more violence and cruelty. A friend who also had a bad childhood quickly joined me, avenging the abuses we had suffered.

A direct hit at the top of the head sent the big hog reeling wildly, but to my surprise, didn't kill him instantly. Blood spurted out of his head in streams of about a foot. I could see his brains through the gaping crack in his skull. Running in circles and squealing, he shook his head from side to side, then finally careened into the fence, fell into a mud-wallow and bled to death.

He was one of many victims killed by Leonard and me, as we made weekly raids on the slaughter house under the nine-span, steel bridge. We had nick names. I was Blinky because I needed glasses and he was Moscow because his parents came from Russia. How curious that I would later hunt Russian boar in earnest, as an adult.

The covert operations of Blinky and Moscow were well planned and always carried out under cover of darkness. Stacking wooden crates into a pyramid

The Alabaster Boy

allowed us to haul up 16 inch cinder blocks to the top of a 12 foot wooden fence, waiting silently for a pig to come and rub against the fence. When that happened we became World War II bombardiers in our imaginations. Once he was in our sights, the bombs-away signal was given under the bridge and another mission was accomplished, leaving us ecstatic with glee as we ran home. We hated everyone and everything, including ourselves and our broken homes. Do yourself and your children a favor: take them hunting and fishing and teach them about the nature of things.

Once I went to the 12 foot fence of the slaughter yard in broad daylight…under the bridge and saw a hog feeding on one of my latest victims, sucking, snorting, pulling and chewing guts and intestines out of his anus. I walked away from that scene no longer a 15 year old boy.

A natural progression from animal cruelty was striking back at humans by serving them up a little cruelty. This was done by breaking into someone's garage and stuffing a pipe bomb down the gas tank of their car. Within seconds everything blew up, as I escaped into the darkness. It was good, but I needed something bigger and more daring, so I began setting fire to railroad cars, by using my home made pipe bombs, of course. An occasional abandoned warehouse was always a treat. I wasn't a pyromaniac, just a kid whose wounds of abuse wouldn't heal, so I found avenues of expressing my anger. So far I had not directed that anger towards any human beings, aside from fighting with other teenagers. So far.

Meeting a three time loser from reform school was all I needed to push me over the top...into the big time. This new friend: Philip had heard about my expertise in explosives, so I gave him a demonstration one night by blowing up another car. "That's pretty good Joe, but why not steal the car, use it for a job and dump it? That way, we make money instead of just getting kicks." The trap that would catch me was set.

The Alabaster Boy

During two weeks of September, 1962, we stole two cars every night and drove to a pre-selected gas station around midnight. Why *two* cars? If one got caught, the other would get away, so we thought. It was a real rush being inside the gas stations, breaking vending machines and pay phones and pilfering cash registers. One night, a cop was making his rounds and pulled into the gas station we were inside of. Winter was on our side, making the broken window look normal, with the corners frosted. He shined his light and moved on, as we watched from the dark corners inside. WE got away with a little over 50 dollars apiece, dumped the cars that were hidden behind the gas station and made it back in to East Chicago, Indiana, where we celebrated with cheeseburgers and coffee at an all night restaurant, situated on one of the four corners of downtown. Ironically, it was across the street from the 1st National Bank, where I used to go and worship the bullet holes, still there from John Milliner's famous robbery 35 years before. The other irony was that only cops and gangsters visited the Indiana restaurant at those hours. Us being the exception. We could hear police radios calling cops to investigate two stolen and abandoned cars. The ones we had just left. Dressed in trench coats and Stetson hats, we looked older, throwing off suspicion, or so we thought.

During the next week, we stole money and other booty from vending machines. The room of my apartment was filled up with grocery bags of cigarettes, candy bars, tools and everything else we could carry away. In another 3 months, I would have enough merchandise to open an actual store, but one night I violently attacked a drunken, old man, knocking him to the ground and robbing him. A 1958 Chevy with a 4-speed and big engine was also stolen on a whim. I never told the police it was my brother. I upheld my code of silence.

Robbery detectives knocked on the door of the old man's apartment several days later, questioning me and then handcuffing me and taking me to jail. Even

The Alabaster Boy

though afraid, I would not confess, but Phil, being the three-time loser I mentioned earlier...squealed and

I went to the county jail as an adult criminal and waited for a court-appointed attorney to discuss my case with. Three months later a guard called my name, handcuffed me and took me to the downstairs section of the jail. "Sit here," he said. and took me to the downstairs section of the jail. "Sit here", 'he said. "Your lawyer will be around pretty soon. Sure enough, a guy walked in and sat down across from me.

"My name is Nick Synac. I'm your court-appointed attorney".

"Hi. I'm Joseph…"

"Shut up. I *know* who you are".

"But don't you wanna' hear *my* side of the story"?

"No. I wanna' hear how much money you got".

"But you're a pauper attorney. Aren't you supposed to be *free*"?

"Look kid. You want *pro-bono*? Get yourself another attorney. Now how much money do you have or how much can you get before trial"?

"Well, *none* right now".

"What about your father? Does *he* have any"?

"I think so".

"Has he been here to see you? Will he be in court"?

"No."

"Why not? Doesn't he care about you"?

"He said that I got myself into this and I'd have to get myself out, but look, Mr. Synac, I can get a job at a car wash or something, when I get out."

"No good. I'll see what I can do for you once the arraignment is held. Then I'll take a look at your sentence investigation. If it looks favorable, I might get you off light.

Meanwhile, you better start writing to some people who have money. At least enough money to satisfy the judge. Do I make myself clear"?

The Alabaster Boy

"Yes, but I was wondering…"

"You talk too much. What's there to *wonder* about? Pay now or go to prison. We're done here. Guard! Take him back upstairs"

On February 27th, 1963, in Lake County Criminal court, Crown Point, Indiana, my case came before Judge John G. McKenna.

"Has the defense had adequate time to prepare its case."?

"We have your honor."

"And how does the defendant plead"?

"Guilty and asks that the court to consider he is a first offender and take into consideration that he has just turned 16 years of age".

"Very well. This court sentences you to serve a sentence at the Indiana State Reformatory, the period of which shall not be less than one year, nor to exceed ten years. Next case."

CHAPTER 7—ON THE YARD

"Adult prison is no place for someone who has just turned 16." That's what I thought, until I strained against the shackles and chains to get a look out of the window of the county sheriff's car. There were 30 caliber machine guns hanging out of each guard tower, complete with sirens and spotlights. Trying very hard, I had finally made it to the *big house.* My wish at that time was that the detective's bullets would have found their mark, as he pursued me from the scene of the crime that winter night. Abandoning the stolen car I was in, I ran and dove over an embankment that ran along the side of a narrow creek that was frozen over. Running for my life was almost impossible, as each foot crashed through the ice, into the freezing water. Plodding through the creek was rapidly tiring me, so I hopped up to the top of the other side of the creek and doubled back to find Philip with his hands raised in the air. A marked police car sat next to the detective's car and the two stolen cars, with lights flashing and radios telling the story to the empty night air. Crawling off into the frozen darkness, I sat down in a field to rest and only then reflected upon how careless I had been with my life. All I could remember since birth was running. Running from the terror of violence. Running from love. Running from neighborhood gangs. Running from the police, but most important, running from the past and myself, toward an uncertain future. Now...I had run out. Out of time, as I sensed capture would be soon. I was breathing my last breath of free air at that moment. Arrest came that night, but those crimes were only a mask that covered a deeper crime. I had been committing self abuse, although I didn't realize it at the time. Strike four.

Joseph Anthony

If I served the entire sentence, I would be between 26 and 27 years old when I got out: no longer a young teenager, but a hardened criminal. Being estranged from the love of mom and Elaine for several years added to my guilt and convinced me of being unworthy of forgiveness. "Could it be if dad had stayed in the basement apartment, I would have been more heavily influenced by love, preventing this?" I said "no. I did the crime…I'll pay the time"…and did.

Parents read this chapter then read it to your kids. It is all true and can happen to anyone. That means *you.* Never mind the television serials that glamorized prison life, just take it from one who's been there and seen it all. There is only fear and boredom, just like war. Hours of boredom lull you into thinking everything is calm, when suddenly violence runs through the cell block like an electric current, paralyzing everyone with the fear that *they* might be the next victim of another inmate.

Joseph Anthony was no longer my name. From that first day my new name was #45869. After passing through the inner bars, I was stripped and every body opening was probed for contraband. Then all of the hair was shaved from my arm pits, pubic areas and skull and sprayed with what is called bug juice. It's a de-lousing chemical that burns like fire for 24 hours. You cannot wash it off. It just keeps burning. While your standing there, bald and naked, all of the seasoned cons are checking you out and passing on tips to other inmates. Tips about who is the youngest and prettiest and whose anus will be penetrated first by the largest and most brutal stud in the joint. Locked up in *isolation* for the first 30 days is like solitary confinement. It protects new inmates from general population and visa versa. It also allows a lot of time to get your plan together. The one you're going to use to survive. If you think you were abused *before* then prepare for the revelation of what *real* abuse is, or there's always the option of staying out of trouble…if you've got the guts to stay in school, graduate and work like a good citizen

Joseph Anthony

Back in the isolation cell block, I was marched out 3 times a day for meals. Each time gave the inmate population a chance to give me a good look over. I was in the *fish* line: the one with all the new inmates that moves slowly toward the steam tables, as you hold your spoon and try to hold your courage together, while 2400 hardened bisexuals, homosexuals, he-she's, rapists, child sex offenders, masochists and sadists salivate over weird hopes and desires of doing things to you that are beyond horror and beyond your imagination.

While waiting in line, grown men whistled at me and taunted me. In their eyes, I was one of three things. Not a person, but a thing. Either I performed oral sex or received anal sex like a woman receives a man.

That is known as being a *punk*. There is one last classification: the stool-pigeon/snitch/informant. They are usually killed soon after being released from isolation. Sometimes before. There is a network in prison that can 'reach out and touch you.' anytime they want. And for you really tough guys, who were what

The Alabaster Boy

you call gangsters, while on the street, I have big news. Your Barrio brotherhood, Arian brotherhood, Skinhead Neo Nazi organization, or Black Moslem groups are not going to budge one inch to help you when you are attacked. You will have to win and *then* they *might* support you. *My* number one responsibility was staying alive, even if it meant someone else would die. That was the plan I formulated while in the isolation cellblock.

In addition to being issued 2 complete sets of clothes, I was issued a large soup spoon. If lost, I would eat the rest of my meals with my hands. Nevertheless, I spent every night of isolation sharpening my spoon's edges on the concrete floor of my cell, which was five feet wide, 8 feet high and 10 feet long. The spoon soon had edges at least sharp enough to slash. You see, you never stick. Always slash an opponent. That way maximum damage will be inflicted. A man that's been stuck could come after you, but not one that's been slashed, cause' his guts will most likely be hangin' out.

Joseph Anthony

When the cell doors were opened, it was for meals, yard time exercise or work. The rules were walk in a marching, straight line and maintain absolute silence. Talking in line drew 3 days in solitary confinement. Talking back to a guard drew 30 to 60 days in solitary. Food in solitary was one piece of bread and a cup of water in the morning, one spoonful of beans and a piece of bread for lunch and 1/2 cup of soup at night.

Marching in line back from mess hall one morning, another inmate shouted, "the new white boy's ass is mine." I quickly responded, "there's only one thing worse than a punk and that's a nigger punk, so dream on you black bastard." Johnnie L. was walking next to me and said, "get ready, he'll try to hit you in the stairway." When he pulled his knife, Johnny stepped in and smoothed things over, or I would have died right there on the stairway. My survival plan had not worked too well.

The next morning I went before the transfer board and was assigned to the furniture factory, then to

The Alabaster Boy

the paint factory, where all the yellow and white lines you see on the highways come from. At lunch in mess hall, I ran all this down to Johnny. He said, "remember the guy on the stairwell? He works in the paint factory. Watch out...he'll try to get you." He *did* try one day, but I ran, escaping his wrath. A few days later, someone attacked him with a pair of shears, while he was sitting on the toilet, chopping up his stomach until his intestines fell out before him, becoming a final resting place for his head, as he toppled over and died with his face buried in his guts. Sound glamorous yet to any of you street *gangstas?*

Yard guards blew their whistles and everyone was put on lock down, which means being marched immediately back to your cells and locked down until the murder is investigated. In the early, dark of morning, I heard Johnnie's voice from down at the end of the tier. "Joe...there's his coffin. Look." In front of the cell block, a wooden box was carried to the rear gate, which was the first time I ever saw outside the 35 foot walls.

Joseph Anthony

He was buried in the prison cemetery. As his cheap wooden box was transferred, every spotlight of every guard tower was covering every cell block and every tower guard walked the top of the wall, ready with their scoped, 30-06 rifles, while their shift partners manned the .30 caliber machine guns. Why? Because every time a con is killed, every other con dies vicariously and his short-term reactions may result in a riot. I remember the crunching sounds of each pallbearer's footsteps in the frozen snow, as they carried the body outside the prison walls, where the old, black convict finally found freedom. He wanted sex and got killed.

Most younger convicts, like myself, lived in 'H' cell house and had more gym recreation time than the older cons. It was there in the Quonset hut gym that I met old Benny, once a light-heavyweight contender, now serving life. In our first sparing match, with about 600 inmates watching, I knocked him down twice during the first round. Embarrassed, he trained me daily for 1 1/2 years, polishing off all the rough edges until no one

The Alabaster Boy

would fight me. I had arrived as someone, who on the outside\ could easily be a contender. Thanks to Benny, I emerged not as a 118 pound, skinny and unskilled youth, but a sculpted, 149 pound junior middleweight who knew how to direct every ounce of weight to the critical or kill points of any opponent. After that first night in the ring with Benny, not one person bothered me again. Later, old Benny's body couldn't live any longer and I mourned his passing, along with many other boxers he had trained. I also watched *his* coffin being carried out of the rear gate. Everyone respected him and did not leave their cells for breakfast that morning, out of respect. You could hear the Springtime birds singing his eulogy.

Parents, tell your children *this* also: *My* heroes were *real* gangsters like Al Capone, Lucky Lucciano, Dutch Shultz and the rest of the Mafioso, now called Coosa Nostra. They all went down, but In any given week, the Godfather's who control America could give orders to completely wipe out the Bloods, Crypts, Posse

Joseph Anthony

and every other punk gang trying to make headlines. The only really tough guys are dead, doing time or are on death row.

An incidental word to all of you tough guys who feel you can commit any crime and fall back on a defense of being abused: there are attorneys who are much smarter than you and specialize in prosecuting people just like you. Don't tell me I'm wrong, because even though I got out in 1 1/2 years, a prosecutor made sure I got a 10 year stretch. I was abused too, but it was not a defense. Abuse wasn't even on the medical/social horizon yet. Domestic violence was common and kept in the closet back then.

One day the medics came running to 'H' cellblock, trying to save a Naphtha (lighter fluid) freak, who had sniffed too much. It was too late. He had sniffed so much that the tiny air sacks in his lungs were eaten throughout by the powerful chemical. Similar to sniffing glue. Since his tiny air sacks were destroyed, they could produce no air to keep the chemical out, so he choked to death on his own blood, which filled his lungs and drowned him.

At night, after *lights out* I heard the lonely sounds of trains passing me by. They were on their way to somewhere, while I was going nowhere. There is nothing worse than seeing, smelling or hearing… freedom, when *you* are not free. Loneliness is horror.

It has caused me great mental anguish and physical suffering to tell this whole story, so I will end this chapter telling you that there were hundreds of things that happened to me while I was in prison, which I don't wish to mention. My best advice is don't go there.

CHAPTER 8—THE GAUNTLET

Having served 1 1/2 years of a 10 year sentence, I was 17 years and 4 months old when released on parole and in their wisdom the parole board decided I should return to high school as a sophomore. That was mistake number one. They also decided I should return to live with my old man. That was mistake number two. Had they known about the daily abuses I experienced since early childhood, perhaps they would have put me in some sort of halfway house, but they had unwittingly set the stage for the final conflict.

After being home only two days, a special semester was created for me to re-enter high school.

The Alabaster Boy

Home for supper after the first day of school, I sat down to a bowl of soup that I had dipped for myself. With head bowed, I was silent, while watching Johnny and the old man out of the sides of my eyes, just as I ate while in prison. If I said or did the slightest thing wrong, the old man would call the parole officer and have me sent back, so I had remained silent since arriving from prison.

Attempting to use some of the Dale Carnagie diplomacy I had learned, I finally spoke. "This soup is really nice. I didn't get anything like this while I was in the joint." I meant it as a complement, an ice breaker, even though it had the same sour, spoiled taste it had always had. "Nobody invited you to go there, you miserable little c___s___r", he responded. The quick fists I had developed and the hair-trigger temper built in prison flashed within me, but only for a moment. What really made my blood boil was the name he called me, which he also called everyone else. But it had a different meaning to *me,* after fighting off all of the sex freaks for a year and a half. I could feel the storm brewing, but wasn't *ever* going back to the joint for *anyone.* Especially him. Hitting someone suddenly is called *firing* on them, in prison jargon. At that moment I was coiled like a snake, ready and able to fire on him, for prison had taught me how to reason like a grown man. I was almost 18 going on 35 and now was not the time. I would wait, get my release from parole and see what happened. Meanwhile, without income, I attended school all day in my prison clothes: the suit given me by the state.

Classmates seemed silly-headed and full of puppy love, while I was on the prowl for women and considered *them* children. I thought people feared me back in the days of Tony's pool hall, but now realized that people were staying away from me in crowds. The word must have gone out that I was now an ex-convict and now that I didn't want anyone to fear me...everyone was *really* scared of me, including every single teacher, the dean, principal and coaches.

The Alabaster Boy

There were many reasons for hating my new school mates. They were little adolescents who had Jello and cream pies for school lunch, while I walked around the block during lunch hour, or met with my parole officer. When kids saw me meeting with a real life, FBI type, it must have sent a signal. Every afternoon, they went to little parties and had colas and chips at someone's house, where the mother provided doilies. I went home to another pot of spoiled slop, usually some sort of cabbage soup. I guess it never dawned on the old man that other boys and girls were eating normal food. Then one day I figured it out, after looking at his bankbook. He wrote $300 dollar checks every two weeks for booze, but not one entry for a single dime for Johnny or me had ever been made. That's when I began to understand him. He was a typical alcoholic, who knew he would lose his job once he went on a bender, and as a precaution, built up a safety net of $2,300 to buy booze. Winter was coming on and I landed a job at a truck stop, fueling diesels and washing their windows at night, while attending school by day.

Upon my parole officer's next visit at high school, I begged him to let me get a G.E.D. diploma at night, so I could get away from my younger classmates and earn some money to buy clothes and decent food. He agreed. The senior girls looked to me like fresh meat to a Grizzly bear and I could smell trouble coming. Besides, I couldn't stand all of those little whimps being terrorized, while they tried to play high school heroes by sporting their sweaters with letters on them. They were only beginning to get a glimpse of real life, while I had already seen men murdered over the sexual favors of a joint *queen*, or commit suicide or be ripped to pieces as they tried to go over the wall and the guards shot them, their bodies dropping to the ground in a heap.

Soon after I got the truck stop job, an old acquaintance from my former days stopped by with a guy who I heard was dating the girlfriend who had waited for me while I was in prison. He gingerly made

The Alabaster Boy

his way up to me while I was filling a truck and tried to explain how it was all a mistake. Gregg: the guy with him, kept saying, "oh yeh, that's right, Joe. He never did anything while you were gone." The other guy's name was Bob. Without warning, all the hatred seething inside me surfaced and in one swift motion, I hung up the gas pump, spun around with a right hook and knocked him unconscious beside the truck. Gregg was stunned and kept saying, "you really lifted him off the ground, Joe." He said it 3 or 4 times until finally I grabbed Gregg by the front of his shirt and said, "He was lying and so are you. Go around the neighborhood and tell everyone I'm back…as a man and I'm not playing any little kid games like back when we all *thought* we were tough. I pulled him even closer to me until our noses touched and said, in a graveled voice, "Now we're not going to tell any cops about this *are* we? Put him in the car and don't' come back." End of dialogue.

One night, after a rough shift, I walked from the truck stop to Jo-Jo's drive in. One of the waitresses called my now fiancée a whore, so I decked her too. It didn't matter to me, because I had hurt or tried to kill everything that walked, crawled, swam or flew. Of course, I was in the Hammond, Indiana jail the next day, because Cindy, the slut I punched, was the favorite niece of Captain Carter: Chief of Detectives. Prior to that, I had spotted an old acquaintance named Sammy, from the joint. Sammy had been a woman or a *punk* in the joint, out of fear and was now sitting in a car trying to impress some broad, which infuriated me, so I walked up to the driver's seat and told ol' Sammy's girlfriend that he was a bisexual. Sammy pulled a gun. I left. That's smart. My parole officer warned if I got in a fight with another man, it was over.

"Well, you didn't hit another *man*. Instead you hit a woman. Now Captain Carter has agreed to let this issue drop and I'm stretching out on a limb by saying you didn't hit another man. Be good and I'll be around to see you," but he didn't come around to see *me*. Instead he visited my *father-in-law* to be, letting the entire cat

The Alabaster Boy

out of the bag: quite a different story than his daughter told him, saying I had been in California for a couple of years. I apologized and he graciously accepted, as his own, youngest son had been in trouble too.

In the year and a half I was incarcerated, my so-called girlfriend visited twice to tell me she was going out with other guys. My brothers visited once and so did the old man, with the only motivation being to find out if I was the one who joy rode his newest car and put a dent in it. I was already in jail by the time he got his new car and told him so. Infuriated at being outsmarted, he tried to lunge at me to get his hands on my throat.

In a micro second, a guard was right there to stop him and inform him that I was no longer a little boy he could attack at will, but a man who was a convict, who the prison would protect. "You gonna' come to the parole board hearing in December, or put in a good word for me," I asked? He responded by gritting his teeth and saying, "you got yourself in…you get yourself out." I rose and turned away without a word.

Joseph Anthony

Earning my G.E.D. diploma, I continued work at the truck stop. Still a ward of the *old man's,* I got home after each shift as soon as possible, but couldn't shower or bathe to get the smell of the diesel fuel off, because the old man's sleep would be disturbed. Neither was I allowed to open the refrigerator to get something to eat after 8 hours of work. The first and last time I tried to eat, the old man stormed out of his room in his underwear with a glazed look of hatred in his eyes, announcing, "there ain't gonna' be any damn midnight snacks around here. From now on, you pay me for food and this apartment." Johnny and I both already made enough to oblige him, so we each paid him $80 a month for rent and bought our own food, which he gladly helped himself to, because it was normal food: something he would never dream of buying for himself. We paid a total of $160 dollars a month for rent and the apartment only cost him $40 a month. Tensions were running at an all time high, as Johnny and myself grew to 19 and 20 years of age.

The Alabaster Boy

Still working our jobs, we tried so very hard to live in peace with the *old man,* who true to form, had been going on drunken benders more frequently than before, but *now* there was no more mama or devoted Elaine to intercede on our behalf.

When Johnny and I arrived home after midnight, the club downstairs, comprised of men who were 25 to 30 and older, was going full force, but the landlord wasn't there and the club's fierce reputation made any do-gooder think twice about calling the cops. In fact, Mr. Landlord was also too terrified to say a word. With all that noise going on nightly, the *old man* was smart enough to know that a gunshot, inside an apartment, would never be noticed.

He kept a sawed-off, double barrel shotgun in his closet and slept with two handguns under his pillow, just *hoping* someone would try to break in…so he could kill them. We locked the door at night, only to hear him get up and unlock it.

Joseph Anthony

Showering at the truck stop washed the diesel fuel from my body, but not my clothes, which I put in a plastic bag as soon as I got home. One morning, while sleeping on the mattress I shared with Johnny, I was suddenly awakened by the old man viciously kicking me in the ribs over and over, while he screamed, "get up you f____n' skunk! You're trying to *force* me to murder you, aren't you? Well, I think you finally made it." Reaching for the gun in his pocket, I could see he was out of control and I was out of patience, jumping up in his face, ready to attack. "This time, old man, you got right out on the edge," I said in a deliberate, ice cold voice. (I *also* slept with a pistol under *my* pillow, but it was now in my hand.) "Pull that hardware all the way out of your pocket and lay it on the floor," I demanded. "I don't have no damn gun," answered the *old man.* "Well, you better dig one up," I threatened. "Oh…here it is, in my back pocket…heh-heh. Didn't even know I had it on me," he sheepishly remarked. "Put it on the floor," I demanded for the last time, "unless you want

The Alabaster Boy

to cross over the edge." He put it down and the whole matter was over as quickly as it began. I dressed, left the house and didn't' return until Johnny arrived after 11 p.m. It was supposed to have been my day off and the next day was to be Johnny's day off.

When I arrived, Johnny was resting on the mattress, watching T.V., as the old man came to, after sleeping off on an all day drunk. I told Johnny what happened that morning and to be on the alert for mood swings and loaded guns. It took weeks for my ribs to heal.

The *old man* got up and changed the channel. Johnny changed it back and the fight was on. The *old man* grabbed Johnny by the hair, trying feebly to shake his head back and forth. Johnny punched him, knocking him across the room back into his chair. Overpowered, the *old man* was not about to be upstaged, so rushing to the kitchen and grabbing a chair to reach the cabinets above the refrigerator, he grabbed a handgun. Johnny and I rushed him like 2 linebackers, with all 3 of us ending up on the floor scrambling for the gun. I tore it loose while Johnny grabbed the other pistol and sawed-off shotgun from the bedroom. We kept the guns for several hours, ignoring the *old man's* glare until we left…unloading all firearms and dumping them on the kitchen table, as relics are left after a cease fire is declared after a long-fought war. *Our* war was over…but not his. He would fight his demons until he was murdered.

Remember, for *your* sakes, the phrases the old man used during the early years? "You're trying to *force* me to kill you, aren't you?" Remember his edict of not eating until he said so? How about grabbing my mother by the hair and throwing her across the room? Sound like anyone grabbing Johnny's hair? A little thinking shows that a leopard never changes its spots. Neither did the *old man.*

Several months prior, while drinking, the leopard told me about Mexican Joe: the man who used to till the ground with my *old man's* tractor back in California.

The Alabaster Boy

The tractor came up missing, but a few days later mysteriously appeared...*without* Mexican Joe who was murdered by the *old man*. Number two and three were steel workers at Inland Steel in East Chicago. "I clubbed them with a pipe wrench and shoved both of them into a furnace," he said. "They p____d me off, that's why." While a merchant marine, he sailed the Great Lakes, beat another guy to death and dumped him overboard. Was this just the alcohol talking? If the disappearance of Mexican Joe is any indication, it was more than just talk.

CHAPTER 9—MARITAL ABUSE

Seeking a life *free* of abuse, I made the most common mistake of the male gender: thinking with the head of my penis, rather than the one on my shoulders, which led me straight into an ill-fated marriage at the age of 19. There *were* two wonderful blessings; however; from out of that marriage: a son and daughter whom I will always treasure. In time, her selfish nature would find a way to take even *them* from me, when there was nothing more to take.

Many do not realize that there are countless numbers of abused *husbands* because most think of physical dominance as belonging to the male. According

The Alabaster Boy

to statistics from the * *National Domestic Violence Hotline*, that's true in 92% of the cases, but I didn't dare lay a hand on her for two reasons. One, the superior athletic conditioning coupled with my boxing skills would have killed here and secondly, I was determined that neither she nor the children would ever know what abuse was. That resolve held firm throughout the entire marriage, although *she* saw no reason to restrain herself from anything she wanted to do to me, the children or anyone else. So it was that I became part of the * 8% club of abused husbands.

Let us begin with sexual abuse, which started on our very first night together, in the wedding chamber of our bed. I was not allowed to reach a climax, but instead was pushed off of my bride with all of her strength just a few seconds before. I didn't know anyone could be so cruel. *My* seed wasn't planted that night, but the seeds of *distrust* were, when she tried to cover her lie about being pregnant. "Maybe I'm not pregnant. Uh, I mean, there's a chance". I saw through her deception. She was just out of high school and wanted a meal ticket. Throughout our marriage, it was I who had to please first, with her seldom reciprocating, leaving me to cope with rejection and real physical pain. Allowing obesity to overtake her was another form of sexual abuse that made me sick, rather than excited. Newlyweds are never pictured that way when the little statues of the bride and groom are placed atop the wedding cake. Oh, there was sex on occasion, but never love making and if I didn't want to she usually came up with a physically or mentally brutal attack. What does the *law* call forcing someone to have sex by use of violence? Is rape too strong of a word?

Working two full time jobs and a part-time weekend job landed us a brand new home in the suburbs. Hoping against hope, I thought this would breathe some new life into our marriage, but daily our relationship became more like the front line of a battle field. For a while there was quiet, punctuated every so often by her violent outbursts. Soon it was violence almost always. My friends, that is not love. It is merely putting up

The Alabaster Boy

with one another. She knew I would not respond to her violence with more violence, so in *her* mind she was tougher than me and could brutalize me at her slightest whim.

Out of many physical attacks, three extremely violent ones typify her and stand out in my mind. Once, after a protracted argument, I had to leave the house or lose my temper. It could not be the latter. On my way out, with my back turned to her, she threw a butcher knife at me, intended for my back; however, the grace of God guided its path to my left hand, which was upon the door jamb. I turned to see what manner of evil spirit had caused her to try to kill me, but her eyes were dead-looking, revealing nothing but hatred. Driving to the police station was my only option. If it happened once, it would happen again and maybe next time would be the last for me. "Do you want to swear out a warrant against her for attempted murder," the policeman asked? "No. I couldn't stand to see my babies without a mother," I replied. "Then we'll bandage your wound.

Joseph Anthony

Try to see a doctor and try to make peace at home," said the officer. The whole thing took about three hours, so when I arrived home her temper was somewhat abated, but not her attitude. Perhaps there were things in *her* childhood that compelled her to behave so irrationally. "So what happened," she asked? I told her the story. "Oh, so now *I'm* the one with the criminal record and they let the ex-con go as the victim. Maybe now you'll think twice before you walk out in the middle of an argument," she said. "Don't worry…there won't *be* another time, because I refuse to argue with you anymore." No response came forth, because she was satisfied with winning the fight. But I, as a real life fighter, knew that no one ever wins a fight. To this day she has never learned that truth. I went to the doctor the next day and had the wound re-dressed.

Three weeks later, a minor argument erupted, causing her to hurl a coffee cup at me, striking me in the right side of the head. Becoming light headed, I fell to my knees, asking her to get a towel so I could stop the

The Alabaster Boy

bleeding. "Get it yourself, big tough boxer," she snarled. As my head cleared a little, my vision became sharper. Recognizing too much blood was pouring out of my head, I grabbed a towel *myself,* while she watched TV. Wrapping my head, I drove straight to the hospital and the same doctor attended, who took care of me the *last* time. "Joseph," he said in a *very* serious voice. "This cannot continue. Either you have your wife thrown in jail, at *least* for one night, or return home and take your chances. She's psychopathic. This is a *serious* wound. It required 23 stitches. The choice is yours. Maybe next time the coroner will see you." I didn't want to die, but each successive attack became more serious. Wondering what I would do when the next one came, brought ungodly thoughts. "Four body blows would break her ribs and puncture her lungs. Another shot to the backbone would shatter her spine. Once down on the floor, I could kill her with one jarring, smashing blow to the nose." Reason took over and I dismissed those thoughts, hoping some untimely accident would cause her death. The doctor was right. It *was* getting serious. Too serious. *Again* I had no options. Her temper was now totally unrestrained, as well as her sexual appetite, physical appetite for all the wrong foods and of course, avarice and greed accompanied them, so no matter how many jobs I worked, I could never bring home enough money for her to fondle and delight in. Gluttony has no bounds.

A decision was made by me, to quit my job as a spray painter and go to work at United States Steel, to begin a career as a design drafter. Initially, there was a salary drop, but the promise of raising myself to the professional ranks of business would pay off in 5 to 10 years. She worried constantly about the lack of money *then,* and to this day is a prisoner of the *love* of money.

Bringing home work at night to get ahead in the company was commonplace, but 'me, myself and I' was all she felt. It was on one such occasion that she marched up to the kitchen table and demanded I cease my evening work and pay attention to her. Did I forget

The Alabaster Boy

to mention that she had a loaded 12 gauge shotgun pressed against my head in order to make her point? Able to summon up all of my courage from the old prison days, I simply said, "go ahead and shoot. Being dead will be better than being with you. Besides, what are you going to tell little Joey and Debbie when the shot wakes them up and they come running in here to find their mother had just splattered their father's brains all over the kitchen wall? Now unload it and put it away. You will *never* force me into having sex with you again at gun point or by any other threats"! End of story? Not yet, because although sexual abuse and physical violence cause *physical* pain, only specific acts of cruelty, usually premeditated, target the most sacred realms of a human: the *emotional* world. Those who seek to wound or destroy such a fragile environment are themselves, usually without emotion, at least for everyone else but themselves. In other words, they're just mean and delight in the suffering of others. That is sadistic.

Joseph Anthony

To the point, we were invited to my eldest brother's house for Easter dinner. My sister-in-law had prepared a wonderful feast. There was ham, polish sausage, salads, desserts and much more. Edmund Jr.: my eldest brother happened to spot a length of hair on one of the sausages at the same time I did, but my ex-wife had already far exceeded the boundaries of shear gluttony. As she reached for the hairy sausage, we didn't have a chance to stop her, before she swallowed it whole, like a python snake swallowing a whole pig in one gulp. Somehow she pulled the hair out, while Ed and I turned red, trying not to laugh. I guess she thought it was *my* fault, so she took a heaping plate of food and rubbed it in my face. With tears of embarrassment, I left the table. "I'll bundle-up the kids and wait in the car," I said.

Eight months later, while visiting her Uncle Julius and Aunt Leana, the telephone rang and the ex-wife was always the first in line for something that might be a real juicy tragedy. Answering the phone,

The Alabaster Boy

she talked for several minutes then returned to the living room. Her eyes were wild with excitement at the prospect of being the first to say, "Joe your dad is dead! She was grinning, waiting for me to break. It could have been said in a more gentile manner. Uncle Julius looked at her and said, "My God. Did you *have* to tell him *that* way?" This was commonplace in her behavioral pattern. The next night while lying in bed, the shock took over and I began to cry. "Go sleep on the couch if you're gonna' do *that*," she insisted...so I did. Uncle Julius said to me, "when you cry...you always cry alone," as I did at night for the next week or so. To make matters worse, I hired a private detective, who proved that my father's death was murder, even though the county coroner called it accidental death. "Well, your dad was just another drunk, so who cares," the ex remarked. It was Christmas when she said that.

At one time I could see my future as amber waves of grain, flowing freely in the summer breezes of happiness, providing bread for whoever needed a boost in life. I wanted enough to live, but also enough to give. *Her* attitude toward those who needed the bread of life was just like that of Marie Antoinette: "let them eat cake."

Leaving the relationship shortly thereafter and giving 95% of my money to her lawyers, she salivated for the coup de grace of emotional destruction, which came soon as she took my children until they were eighteen. The choices I was given was either give more money, which I didn't have, go to jail and waste away on alimony row, or sign adoption papers, which meant I could never see them again. That is, unless my two children would care to look me up when they turned eighteen years old.

Now out of the new suburban home I had built for them, I struggled to mend my torn emotions and start a new life. One that would be a stranger to abuse, but all the king's horses and all the king's men couldn't put me back together again. I was 24 years old and began to

The Alabaster Boy

fall into a pattern of heavy drinking, self abuse and self punishment.

I found a boarding room for $10 a week and spent $11.88 every Monday on groceries, made up mostly of lunch meat ends that the butcher would have thrown out anyway. Depressed, I soon moved to another town, another state and eventually, another state of mind. Guilt-ridden and grieving over the loss of my children, the pattern of self abuse became more severe. Drinking and bar room fights filled every lonely evening.

Occasionally, I would enter the men's room of a bar and punch myself in the face until my cheekbones and eye brows were swollen and black. Finally I abused myself financially, by trading in a good engineering job for a pair of 8 ounce boxing gloves. Clouded judgment told me I could be the next middleweight champ of the world, instead of a draftsman. Strike five.

Tony Zale fought Rocky Graziano 3 times for the middleweight crown. These fights were called the Blood baths of the Century. The once great fighter watched me work out at Navy Pier in Chicago one night. Punchy and assisted by his wife, he rambled on about the past until Mrs. Zale spoke up. "You're pretty good Joey, but too old. Tony took the title when he was 28. You're the same age and just *starting*. I suggest you go to Vegas and pick up some money fighting smokers and club fights. Thanking them for their time, I waited until they left, then without dressing walked out to the end of Chicago's famous Navy Pier. Standing only in boxing trunks and boots, I wiped the tears from my cheeks and shouted defiantly at the freezing winds and sleet that pelted me. "I am *not* too old! I *am* tough enough! I *will* be champ! I *hate* that punch-drunk old fool and his goofy old lady too. You're not so tough," I shouted to the burning cold of Lake Michigan. "I hate you too. I hate everyone and I'll *kill* anybody that tries to stop me…in or out of the ring." With beads of workout sweat now frozen to my body, I screamed out like a wild animal, "I am somebody"! Over and over my voice, driven by extreme hurt and hatred, echoed

The Alabaster Boy

across the lakefront until I convinced myself that all of my words were true.

Changing into warm clothes, I left the pier and the next morning phoned my 3 girlfriends to say good-bye, leaving my car to one of them. There was a Chicago business man who hired drivers to deliver new cars across the country. I drove one to Phoenix and caught a plane to Vegas, dreaming of the glory I would have in the sacred, square arena of modern day gladiators.

My airborne dreams were interrupted once or twice, by ugly nightmares of suicide attempts. Every time I tried, though, I envisioned my little Joey and Debbie standing over their daddy's casket. That would've scarred them forever. Maybe they would see me boxing on TV and Howard Cosell would let me say a couple of words to them, I hoped. Oh how I hoped too much, I now know. When you're desperate, your mind will come up with the most bizarre fantasies. It's a survival mechanism that kicks in automatically to make things bearable.

The Alabaster Boy

CHAPTER 10—VEGAS-THE OPENING ACT

Boxing soon took a back seat to the glitz and glamour of Vegas. Daily beatings at the Ringside Gym simply weren't as much fun as lounge shows, gambling and fast women who were even faster with their favors.

Almost every apartment complex in Vegas has a swimming pool. I met Sandy at my pool and within a half hour, knew her intimately. For the next four days and nights, I keep her in her bed, except to break for a meal or two. By then she would do anything for me. She was a tennis pro at the Hilton and knew some

The Alabaster Boy

celebrities like B.B. King, the famous blues musician and Bill Cosby. B.B. handed me a roll of bills and told me to go to a gym in the Watts section of L.A. There I met a trainer named Candy, who trained the renowned Sugar Ray Robinson. He was blind in one eye from an old boxing injury, but still knew who as championship material.

That was one of the greatest days in my life. I still recall the smells and sounds of a real, old fashioned gym. One with wooden floors, where the rhythms of the jump rope made a tapping sound twice a second. Two rings were set up back to back. Fighters sparred all day long. Speed bags were a blur, as hands taped in white propelled them into perfect timing, make them sing out in a rat-a-tat timing…like a tap dancer. Boom boxes belted out songs to help the boxer's rhythms. Add the sound of leather gloves slapping and thumping the heavy bags. Throw in the ringing bells that count off each 3 minute round. Above all, remember the spit buckets that catch the fighter's mouth rinse, blood and even teeth. All of these go into making a REAL fighter's gym. Not a Yuppie-type place where men lift weights only to get bulging muscles and pick up chicks. I'm talking about a *fighting* place. An arena of combat where the winner is the one left standing. It was like being in the training camp of Spartacus, back in the days of the Roman empire.

That day, I left, a changed man. So confident was I that I walked from Watts to Gardena with my gloves hanging around my neck, hoping someone would challenge me, but nobody did. Candy said, "go home. Train like this every day. Drink a pint of beef blood every day. It makes you mean. Come back in a month and I want you sparring every day."

Back in Vegas, I thought long and hard about my boxing career and realized I needed a trainer who could watch me every day. Tony Zale was a has-been. Candy had about 75 fighters in his stable and I was not a leading candidate.

The Alabaster Boy

Before long, I changed trainers, selecting Bobby and Carmine DeCiccio, who had a very successful stable of fighters. One was a lightweight with a #1 contender record of 70-2: Jesse Martinez, whom they couldn't get a title shot. None for their #10 middleweight: Rocco, either. Not enough juice with the boys, I guess. Carmine said he wanted me to drop some weight and push for the Welterweight title at 147 pounds. I weighted 157 3/4: a natural middleweight, but the DeCiccio brothers already had picked Rocco as their next middleweight hopeful. I could see that I would never be champ of the 160 pound division, as long as I stayed with Bobby and Carmine, so I switched trainers again. Carmine died of cancer shortly thereafter, so it wouldn't have worked anyway.

My new trainer was the famous Brown Bomber: Joe Louis. We had wonderful plans. Joe would train me. A Caesar's Palace accountant would manage the money, so we wouldn't be cheated like Louis was. I would knock out everyone, win the title and we would

Joseph Anthony

all get rich. Only one problem: Joe Louis had a heart attack, went home to Houston and died. A part of me died too, because I loved that old man, even though he was punchy and almost broke, thanks to the Internal Revenue Service and his crooked manager.

About 10 years before, Sonny Liston was allegedly murdered with a forced injection of heroin, after he lost the title to Mohammed Ali. Johnny Tocco was the trainer who brought Sonny from St. Louis to Vegas, so as a last resort, I hired Johnny as my trainer and worked out every day under his watchful eyes at the Ringside Gym.

One day Johnny said, "go down to the State Athletic Commission and get your license. I'll sponsor you." It did not work out because of certain powers that be and most importantly, Johnny never taught me how not to be afraid. Everyone is afraid when they step into the ring. Everyone who is 30 and faces experienced fighters 10 years younger. In addition, I couldn't get the fight doctor to O.K. my medical certificate, even though

The Alabaster Boy

I had sparred nightly with all pro boxers for 3 years. I had become very dangerous and failure fueled a raging, inner anger that would explode at a moment's notice. Anger management was just coming into being during the mid seventies.

One night while sparring with a light-heavyweight, I was caught twice by powerful right hooks. My memory returned 3 days later, along with the reality of failure. It was my last hoorah in the world of boxing and my last chance for any recognition…or so I thought. Depressed, I sought solace in the arms of a beautiful prostitute. You might remember Debbie from the first page of this story. Even though she was Jamie's main squeeze, she moved in with me because Jamie beat her often. She took the abuse rather than work the streets, while Jamie pimped all of his other girls. He was also a small time drug dealer with a big time problem. Being a valet parker for a major casino afforded him the perfect set up for running his drugs and whores. The scenario of this relationship was bizarre. Daily I stood on the steps of the upstairs apartment, watching Debbie walk to the curb to meet Jamie in his 1976, gold, Lincoln Continental, where he gave her the drugs she needed. Afraid of me and my boxing reputation, he would speed off before my temper launched me from the porch toward him. Jamie was providing her with hundreds of dollars in drugs every week and I couldn't even raise grocery money. It was embarrassing for me not to be able to provide the basics, while Jamie made around $4,000 a week at the casino parking lot. It was also embarrassing the casino owner and a man of his standing could not afford to be embarrassed. "We keep *our thing* out of the spotlight," he said to his right hand man. "Between you and me," he continued, I think Jamie should be grateful for the legitimate grand he gets every week for parking cars, but what does he do? Does he even once show me any respect for giving him the job? No! Instead, he's greedy and pushing $4,000 a week in drugs, using *my* valet parking lot as *his* office. That's over $200,000 a year if he keeps it up." His assistant told me that by this time,

The Alabaster Boy

he was pacing the floor. I will call his assistant Vinnie, because I don't know anyone's real name. Knowing or naming real mobsters can be hazardous to your health.

The boss went on. "This is very bad. Very bad. I think Jamie is sick. He needs medicine, so give him a sleeping pill. I don't want negative publicity to draw the attention of the Gaming Commission or anybody else. Understood?" Vinnie nodded yes…"understood."

You might wonder why they would choose a has-been, ex-pug for such a job. It's because they know all of the pro fighters in every city and realize their readiness for violence and their unfulfilled dreams of a championship. In short, they choose someone highly volatile, extremely capable and…a loser. One who is grasping desperately at one last chance to be a winner at any thing. And so it came to be that I was chosen to whack Jamie, winning favor with the boss and taking Jamie's job and his woman at the same time.

A .380 caliber semi-automatic pistol with ammunition was provided, along with a rental car.

Joseph Anthony

The permit to carry a concealed weapon was issued to Debbie, who carried it in her purse, while I carried the gun, always looking for the perfect time to hit Jamie. The perfect time came and I blew the assignment, as you read in the first chapter of this book. I also tried to bomb his car twice, but something went wrong each time. Someone was watching over me and Jamie, but we didn't realize it at the time. One of us would later realize *Who* it was.

Although I called Vinnie for another job and another chance time and time again, there was never a returned call. I had hit bottom. Jamie kept his life, job and Debbie. My boxing career went down the toilet and so did my hope of becoming somebody. Depression quickly took hold again and soon I was a regular at *Uncle Franks Fun House. A* very rough shot and beer joint, complete with customers who where mostly seedy and crooked. I fit in there. I kept telling the lie of being the #10 middleweight contender, unable to accept not being good enough to whip most other boxers. Most

The Alabaster Boy

of the guys at Uncle Frank's believed me. Those who didn't were too afraid to dispute my claim, so I became a hero of the *Fun House*, occasionally knocking out someone for no other reason than to keep my 'tough guy' reputation intact. My reputation not only kept, but got worse, as nightly fist fights took place. One night, while shooting pool, an ex-girlfriend approached me and said her new boyfriend was waiting outside to beat her up and asked if I could help her out. It was a set-up. When I walked out of the bar, he ambushed me, announcing that he was some sort of Black Belt Karate expert. I broke his jaw. So violent was my response to his challenge, that a regular patron called Big Steve, had to pull me off of the poor guy, dislocating my right shoulder in the process. "Sorry", he said, "but you would have killed him and he's not worth it." Today I'm ever thankful that Big Steve interceded.

CHAPTER 11—VEGAS-THE CLOSING ACT

One day a young woman walked into Uncle Frank's Fun House. Although it was her custom to exercise in the morning and fuel her workout with a steak at noon…I had never noticed her. This day would be different for both of us. It was the day I met Margaret, who later became the love of my life. I was acting up, as usual, to get attention, but she saw something different in me and I in her. Soon we were always together for her brunch, because I made sure I showed up every day at the same time she did. I enjoyed her company and was mean and violent to everyone but her, not knowing why.

The Alabaster Boy

As time went on, we became very close friends. Not yet sweethearts, we both acted contented, telling ourselves that our relationship was only platonic. Looking back, we were both lying to ourselves, because we had both suffered personal hurt and were afraid to hope for love again.

Uncle Frank approached me one day, saying, "Joe, I've seen you do artwork on my bar napkins. Can you make some new, better napkins for me?" I responded with enthusiasm, because here was another chance to be somebody. "Sure! I'll do it. How much will you pay me," I asked? "Well...I've always been good to you and, well...you know...your beers could be free for a whole month if you do this for me," he said. Like a fool, I agreed and did, in fact, deliver the master, which he had to take to the printers. He said, "these are not good. I'll get Freddy to do me some new ones. He's a *real* artist." I snapped back at Uncle Frank. "Freddy's not an artist. I *am.* You'll see the difference." Storming out of the bar, I remembered that Freddy robbed a truck load of T-shirts several weeks before. He had a *real* artist come up with a great logo of the Fun House and conned Uncle Frank into thinking they were a creation of Freddy's. Impressed, Uncle Frank bought them all for $3.00 a piece and sold every single one for $15.00 each, profiting $24,000 under the table. Soon the new bar napkins arrived, much to Uncle Frank's delight and much to my chagrin. "Freddy got $6,000 for the tee shirts and I got nothing," I cursed. Incensed, I dragged Freddy off the bar stool and laid him out on a pool table, where he quickly gave me the artist's name, who actually did the work. The artist who robbed me, I reasoned. Now I needed to teach *him* a lesson, but first I would go to my only friend, seeking counsel.

Salvatore *Two Guns* and I hit it off the moment we met and grew to be closer than brothers. Sammy came from a broken home in the heart of Philadelphia's Kensington district. His Sicilian parents instilled a good set of work ethics in him, while they were still a family, but he liked the fast life.

The Alabaster Boy

Margaret was very vulnerable after the suicide of her doctor husband and Sammy brought cheer and new life to her, during a time of great need. When I met them in Las Vegas, Sammy and I sort of understood that it was our job to watch out for all 3 of us. Salvatore always carried a gun in a hip holster and a back up ankle holster. Hence, the nick name *Two Guns*. People called me *Crazy* Joe Anthony. Many was the night that we walked into the Fun House and heard people mutter, "look out, here come *Two Guns* and *Crazy* Joe, because Sammy would shoot at anything and I would joke and laugh about anything…except Margaret.

Uncle Frankie *the butcher* Diomoni and his scheming nephew: Joey *the talker* Diomoni tried to sell 3 or 4 different bars to Margaret, in an attempt to get what little money her late husband left. Joey 'the talker' got his nick-name by slick-talking people out of their money, but it failed when Margaret's Beverly Hills attorney showed up and proved that Uncle Frankie and Joey were *cookin' the books*. Their lawyer was a surly embarrassment to the legal profession and called Margaret and her lawyer horrible names throughout the series of meetings, but Margaret's attorney kept saying, "next point, gentlemen," moving smoothly and destroying the credibility of the Diomonis and John Katatalia. Outmaneuvered by older and wiser thinking, Katatalia began to curse and threaten Margaret and her lawyers. One night John started being obnoxious in a night club Margaret was visiting. When she checked her weapon, he shut up, but that was the beginning of his demise and that of the Diomonis.

Salvatore, myself and Margaret played it close to the vest for the next several years, but things and feelings of the past mellowed out and we and Uncle Frank and Joey lived in harmony, especially when they found out Margaret didn't' have the kind of money they were looking for.

On the day I went to Sammy for advice on the artist problem. He came up with some real wisdom, which was surprising, because he almost always favored

The Alabaster Boy

swift retaliation. "Joe, I think Freddy cheated you, but this artist never did one thing to hurt you. Leave it alone. They'll be other art jobs, just be patient." He was right. I was wrong and would say, "I'm sorry, but I cannot leave it alone because of the money".

Ignoring Sammy's advice, I found the artist's office the next day. Boldly walking in, I asked, "are you Toby: the artist who did the Fun House T-shirts for Fred?" Then, in the most unafraid, peaceful manner, a voice answered with a simple "yes". I tried to unleash the anger I had been feeling, but couldn't. I wanted to blast him. I wanted to get even with him, but something or someone said, "why? He's done nothing to you. He only used the gifts of an artist, which I gave him." Not knowing who was talking to me, I quickly made up an excuse to leave, but before I hit the door, Toby said, "come back when you have more time and I'll show you what an artists' studio looks like."

On the way home I wondered how he knew of my deep desire to become a famous artist. "Was he some sort of physic or was I cracking up.? It didn't matter. I had met a lot of smooth talkin' guys who melted in fear when I confronted them with violence. He would be no different. There would be another time. It would be next time and next time would be *My* time. A time to hurt.

That night and next day, I concentrated all of my efforts on finding out how to become a legitimate commercial artist and thought it strange that the voice I heard told me the same thing Salvatore told me: "He's done nothing to you. He's just an honest artist who made an honest dollar." Deciding to forego my plans of violence, I visited Toby the artist again, but this time with a sincere hope that I might learn to be an artist of his caliber. All of that would happen very soon, but something else would happen first. Something that would not only change my life, but reverse the course I was on and eventually bring me to the place I had always sought. Toby and I talked for a while then he took me for a ride in his Corvette, afterwards taking me to lunch! Except for Margaret, nobody had ever done

The Alabaster Boy

that for me. By the end of the day, he had told me his whole life's story, how he became a successful artist and how good things kept happening to him, as long as he had faith. "It's exciting to hear all these things," I told him, but I got my own religion." In reality, I had none. He kept saying success would also visit, if I did what he did and tried to follow his example. I couldn't see it happening, but it was worth a try, so I agreed and returned to his office.

Toby locked the door behind us and I thought, "O.K., now I get it. This guy's a homosexual and if I go along with him, he'll throw some business my way." At that moment he said, "it's time," and held my hand, pulling us both to our knees, side by side. "You and I are going to pray now", he said. "Oh no," I thought, "A religious nut…even worse than a gay," but I was suddenly praying with him. I remember the exact words he spoke and I repeated: "Dear Father in heaven. I am definitely a sinner, but I want to change. No man comes to you except through Jesus, Your Son, so I ask you

Joseph Anthony

Jesus…please come into my life. Forgive me and save me and I will live the rest of my life for you. Thank You, Lord. I am now yours and You are mine forever." It was a simple but powerful prayer. Covered with sweat and trembling, I noticed rays of light shining through the dark clouds of a typical winter night in Vegas. The unusual part was that they shown through his window, illuminating the office. After a moment of silence, I heard Toby say, "yes Lord," as if answering a command. Later…he told me it *was* Jesus, saying, "watch over Joe. He is going to be one of my special one's. I've called him from his youth to serve Me and now, he has finally responded." All Toby told me then, was "Joe, see that artist's easel? It has 3 legs that support it. *Your* 3 legs of support have to be fellowship, prayer and reading of the bible every day. Now, it's time to call it a day." Leaving the office, good things began to happen immediately and have never stopped in the last twenty years. I'll get into that later on.

The Alabaster Boy

In September of 1997, Margaret and I had been away from Las Vegas for almost 18 years and needed to conduct a business conference in person with our accountant. Off to Vegas we went. After business was concluded, we decided to find out what happened to our old crowd and were shocked. We should not have been. After all, Jesus said Himself, "touch *not* my anointed and do My prophets no harm." Those who did try to harm us, we forgave years ago, but God's laws are unchanging, so those who were evil to us reaped what they had sown. You don't have to believe me, but consider what we found out. Consider the transgressors who *rejected* Jesus and tried to hurt us.

Uncle Frank *the butcher* Diomoni's Cadillac was found with the keys in it at McCarren airport. He had vanished. His nephew: Joey *the talker* Diomoni got 10 years in prison. John Katatalia was horribly burned, but survived the bombing of his Mercedes, parked in front of the court house. Johnny Tocco recently died suddenly. The nameless casino owner lost his casinos and his whereabouts is unknown. His under-boss was kicked out of Nevada by the Justice Department and Finnie, his strong arm man, has faded into obscurity. Jamie the pimp and drug dealer disappeared and Debbie also vanished, but might still be alive. Six others from the *Fun House* died of drug overdoses. Uncle Frankie's son took over the bar, but was convinced to sell. Someone made him an offer he couldn't refuse. Sadly, our friend and advocate: Salvatore *two guns* moved back to Philly and died of brain cancer. We'll miss him, although he, among all of the others had the privilege of having the gospel preached to him almost every night and every day. I believe he is in heaven.

There was another couple from Chicago, who Joey *the talker* Diomoni sold a restaurant and bar to. They were my first commercial art clients, but when I completed the job, Mrs. Scalla would only give me 20% of my legitimate bill. Their restaurant had a 75 foot bar, stocked from floor to ceiling with expensive glassware. Within five minutes of her refusal to pay the full amount,

The Alabaster Boy

the entire bar collapsed, braking every bottle and glass. The bartender and cocktail waitress had a fight and both quit. Finally Joe Scalla shouted, "we're finished" and soon got a divorce. All of it happened in 15 minutes.

None of these people would listen to me, as I tried to tell them of my wonderful experience with Jesus. None but Sammy, so the others eventually perished. Had they all listened to that still, small voice that's inside all of us, perhaps they would have thought about taking the *cure*. Listen close, for this is *your* moment.

CHAPTER 12—SPIRITUAL AND CLINICAL HEALING

On January 12th, 1978, at 5:15 p.m., I prayed what is called 'the sinner's prayer', with Toby the artist leading me. It was right that I prayed that prayer because I *was* a sinner and so are *you*, if you've never surrendered your life to Jesus Christ. But *you* might not be in the condition I was. You might think of yourself as a good person but Jesus said, "there is *NONE* good except God". He excluded Himself, naturally. You might have a wonderful career, an S.U.V., a wonderful house, terrific children, a beautiful spouse and lots of money. But even the richest, without Jesus, are among

The Alabaster Boy

the most miserable. Yet even the poor, *WITH* Christ, are called kings and princes upon this earth. They are called that by God Almighty Himself.

On that very special day in January, I walked out of Toby's office, got into a borrowed car and said immediately, "O.K., Lord. Now I know you're real. I also only have $1.15 to my name. What do I do?" Suddenly, my girl friend's glove compartment popped open, as I hit a speed bump in a nearby shopping plaza. A piece of paper fell onto the floor. It was a certificate for a free, 10 pound, canned ham! Now I had food for my brother and me. "Hey…that was pretty cool, Lord, but what about the commercial artist job I wanted? If you know everything, and I believe You do, then when am I going to be an artist, "I questioned? There was no audible answer from Jesus, but I had a pager and it beeped. Then a voice said, "Hi Joe. This is Pat Everston. Uh…I understand you are interested in doing some artwork. Call me. Toby gave me your number. I'll see what I can do. Bye." Within minutes, it appeared

Joseph Anthony

I had a *real* artist's job with real *paying* clients. Pat was so gracious he gave me a lot of small jobs I could handle at first then gradually let me work on some of the larger accounts, as I developed my skills. Ironically, an old crony from the *Fun House* ran into me one day and asked me to do some promotional work for a restaurant he hoped to start. "Sure," I said. "Here's my card. Stop by my office and we'll kick around a few ideas." A look of surprise told me he recognized me as a *serious* artist, no longer simply a bar bum that doodled on cocktail napkins. Unable to keep himself from gossip, he soon told a lot of people and my *own* jobs began to pour in. Looks like the *cure* had cured me of financial worries. God really came through for me. I had part of an office in a very exclusive part of Vegas, invoices the clients paid on time, letterheads, envelopes, business license and business cards that people took seriously. Soon prospective clients were calling *me* for appointments! My low self esteem had begun to grow into confidence.

The Alabaster Boy

These financial and social healings were great, but at the same time, the Lord's *cure* was daily at work, healing one emotional hurt after another. For instance, the adoption of my children still hurt. I couldn't walk into a department store at Christmas without ending up in the toy department…crying. One day the loneliness of missing my children seemed too much to bear. That's when I sat on the couch and my innermost being cried out loud. "Dear Father, I come to you again with yet another need. I ask you to save my children, even if it means never seeing them again, although I believe I will, because with You…all things are possible." I laid that burden at the feet of Jesus and never again touched it with my thought life. I came to God with nothing but emotional distress and pure faith. He responded to faith, like He always does and about 6 years later my son and daughter were sitting in my Las Vegas apartment… reunited. A further blessing was my daughter prayed with me, like Toby once did, and received Jesus into her heart. Eventually, Deborah came to live with Margaret and I for a while in Las Vegas and Joey Jr. came to live with us when we moved to Denver. The *cure* was working, not only for me, but my children as well.

I knew deep inside that I needed an emotional healing from the sexual abuse I was subjected to as a child. True sexual gratification satisfy our biological urges, but also fulfill our *emotional* needs. After having known enough women in my lifetime, I realized I never *loved* any of them, but craved mostly oral sex and wanted them to crave me for the same thing. Why? Because my father marched me around the room naked, making me think my penis was something to be ashamed of. If it was something to be ashamed of, why did God create me this way? Answer? Because God created male and female and said "this is good." Upon His creation of woman, He said "this is *very* good. She will be man's helper and the two of them shall become one flesh, one mind and one spirit, in agreement with each other." That's what He said and that's what He meant, but men and women, in their lusts, have perverted the innocent beauty of each other's bodies and the Godly feelings that are supposed to be a part of love making. In order to heal my sexual damages, I read the bible to find out the true meaning of a man and a woman and what their proper relationship should be. By *proper,* I do not mean developing a rigid etiquette for the bedroom, as though the royal family would be watching. What's important is being sensitive to the needs of your spouse, finding out what the other's sexual and emotional desires are and gently coaxing them to feel relaxed, comfortable and uninhibited. Encourage your life's partner to openly express their innermost cravings and sincerely tell them that their desires are your desires. Tell them many times throughout each day, how much you love *all* of them: their moods, habits and everything that makes them special. I have also learned to embrace *myself* as being worthy of being loved, and am not ashamed to bear my soul, my deepest desires, joys and fears to my wife. Being responsible financially, showing sincere interest in *her* social interests and encouraging her in

Joseph Anthony

her professional and personal pursuits will enhance your bedroom life, because you are showing her that love-making is making sure she knows you love and care about her every need, as well as having physical gratification. You can never, ever really *know* someone merely through physical intercourse. I learned that all by consulting Jesus through His written Words. Now I do not entertain false feelings of inadequacy. I have a healthy image of my outer, physical appearance, which can only come from a healed, emotional state. Once again, God's *cure* worked. I can truly say, "I love my wife for all she is and she loves me for all the things I am." Thanks to Jesus.

Abuse covers many more areas other than sexual. For example, beatings, violence and verbal abuse, all of which I needed deliverance from, or healing if you will. One morning while shaving, I splashed aftershave lotion in my eye. It burned terribly and automatically I shouted, or rather, started to shout, "Jesus", without saying Christ. I couldn't get the entire phrase out,

The Alabaster Boy

because I now knew him personally, so what came out was, "Jesus uh...help me"! That was the very sudden ending of my cursing days. In the blink of an eye the vulgarity heaped upon me as a child was not even a distant memory. Verbal abuse had just been healed. The demons of my parents were dead, no longer able to rear their ugly heads. To this very day, I have tried with every breath, to display an excellence of speech. Of course I've failed from time to time, which only served to strengthen my resolve. After 26 years, I'm still growing, but have reached the point where former talk has taken a back seat to language I hope will edify edify those I speak to on a daily basis.

Physical abuse of a child most often turns the abused into an abuser. Such was my case, with the exception of my ex wife and children. Violence had become a way of life at an early age and continued into adulthood until I was 31 1/2 years old. How would I get healed of physical abuse? It hurt as a child and continued to hurt during my teen years, especially during my early adult years, although by then I had developed a hard outer shell to cover the extremely damaging memories of my old man's crazed attacks. I tried to conquer the hurt with violence and combat any attacks by others with *extreme* violence, usually winning and sometimes winning too much, when my opponents suffered more than they should have. Even though I accepted the life Jesus offered, I still had the anger and violence boiling inside me, until the day I decided to visit the old Ringside Gym…just to see who some of the latest fighters were. Walking up to the front door, which was covered with bars because it was in a very bad neighborhood, I tried to go inside. Try as I might, I could not move. It was like being paralyzed. I could hear the boxers working out, but I tell you truly…I could not move…*until* God's Holy spirit told my human spirit something. "I don't ever want you to go into that gym again. If you agree, I'll let you go." No sense trying to fight God, so I said, "O.K." and was suddenly able to move. He said don't go in there, but He didn't say don't look, so I found a portion of window that had some of the black paint scraped off. Looking inside, I saw boxing as I never had before. Men were trying to beat each other to death. I saw my old man trying to do that to my mother, her trying to beat him and both of them trying to beat me. It was not of God, for Jesus is the Prince of peace. Turning away, I never looked back and never went back. Feeling like a limp, wet mop, I felt the tension, anger and violence leave my body. Walking to my car, I looked up at the fresh, sunny sky and compared it to the evil blackness of the gym I had spent 3 years in. I was healed of violence, anger and hatred. It was finally over. Without knowing, I had again taken the *cure* for yet another sickness. Actually I didn't do anything except listen to that inner voice we all have. I prefer to say, listening to the Holy Spirit. What I said about an abused child becoming violent includes the inclination to murder. Edmund and Scottie had it and I had it. But it went too, the day I walked away from the gym.

Joseph Anthony

Another thing I know to be true is the power of forgiveness. This was not an automatic, heavenly move on God's part. It was a conscious decision by me. Over a period of time, since turning my life over to Jesus, I thought often about all those who had hurt me. My parents, ex-wife, prison guards, the *boys* in Vegas at the casinos, those in the boxing racket and everyone else I felt a grudge against. It occurred to me that Jesus said, "if you do not forgive those who have wronged you, neither will or *can* your Heavenly Father forgive *you."* I started visiting and calling all of my old enemies, forgiving them and asking their forgiveness, although most didn't understand. I even had the opportunity to call Jamie: the drug pusher and pimp and asked him if he too would like to try on a new life, like I did, but he declined. The point is, I didn't' just forgive all of these people within my heart. I actually took God at His literal word and physically sought these people out. Some people say, "I forgive but I don't forget." God asked me this: "if you *truly* forgive, why do you keep bringing it up?" In other words, if I forgave, but refused to forget...I hadn't truly forgiven. At that moment, I said out loud, "God. I *choose* not to remember those who have hurt me, because remembering will only bring back bad feelings. In addition, I ask You to save, heal and deliver them from any bondage or hurts, just as you have done for me." Even though I was counted *"out"* after five or more strikes, Jesus said *"safe"* and my Father-God owns the stadium!

No matter how much abuse you've been through, you can begin a new life, free of abuse and memories of past abuses, by doing what I did. It worked for me and I'm just an average guy. What do you have to lose by taking the *cure* that Jesus provides? I'll tell you what you have to lose: vengeance, hatred, self-pity, pity from others and lots of sons for not succeeding. But is that what you really want? I don't think so. Why would you want to continue to live in poverty, sickness, disease, lack and want, when you were created to prosper in every area of your life? I mean *thoroughly* furnished in spirit, soul, body, finances and in your social life! You are first and foremost a spirit being. You have a soul (will, consciousness, emotions, thinking capacity and seat of government for all of your actions). You live in a body that houses them; thus making you a 3-part being just as God is. Do you actually think He lives in poverty, sickness, emotional stress, sin, sickness and disease? Impossible, for none of these could even get close to Him after Jesus destroyed all the works of the devil. The Word says He did all things well and to me, all means everything. The choice is yours, but at least it's not *my way or the highway*. There are alternatives. If you feel the path I took is nit for you, that's fine, but at least take *some* path.

Now that you know the spiritual side of healing, let's take a journey to the clinic and discover the benefits of their treatment methods. Please understand that these two methods of healing are not the only ones available, but they are the best and most successful

The Alabaster Boy

routes to recovering your life. Our journey begins in May of 2001.

After twenty four years of a good and wholesome lifestyle, I was stricken with a major heart attack and almost died, but for the efforts of the emergency medical team. Left with an initial bill of 280 thousand dollars meant immediate compromise of our finances. I couldn't work and my wife, who should have been enjoying her retirement, was now forced to go back to working as many hours as possible. To make matters worse, I had always worked as a contract designer. Moving from one state to another was required frequently and put us in a sort of social prison. Not staying at any location long means not making any long term friends. All of the other contract people were in the same boat.

As the financial pressure, boredom and loneliness reached critical mass, my faith broke under the strain. An old pattern reappeared, as I began to frequent some of the local pubs for a few cold ones. "What's wrong with that", you might ask? "Millions do it every day".

Nothing is wrong, but we must guard against abuse of any type. The *few* cold ones soon became more and my life started in a downward spiral.

Within eight months of the open heart surgery, I found myself in a Massachusetts court, charged with drinking while driving. After court, we moved to the country town of Rome, Pennsylvania, where the cost of living was much lower, and so was the stress level, or so we thought.

Despite relocating, the pressures and problems mounted, so I continued on a path of self abuse, drinking more than I should have. Don't get me wrong. I wasn't out there getting hammered every day, but it only takes one day to screw up your life. That day came just six months after my first DUI. That's right. Another one. The one that really got my attention. Pennsylvania displays highway signs throughout the state that contain the following message. "DUI-you can't afford it". I suggest not violating that law. Imprisonment, court costs, fines, parole, community service, driver's school,

The Alabaster Boy

victim impact course, loss of job and income, urine tests for drug screening and counseling were ordered by the court. The one that affected me most significantly was the counseling. Once released from Bradford County Prison, I underwent three sessions of drug and alcohol analysis, followed by a recommendation that I attend a Continued Outpatient Program, consisting of three phases. This is commonly referred to as COP I, II and III.

Northern Tier Counseling has four or five locations, so that's where I went. *Happy camper* is not how you would have described me, as I was now being told what to do by yet another agency. Once I entered the program, however; I became very proactive. My reasoning was that if professional therapists and counselors were spending their time, talents and knowledge on me, I should at least have the courtesy to reciprocate. Paying attention to them, applying *lessons learned* in my daily life and *working the program* is exactly what I brought to the table and guess what happened? The program worked for me. That is how my life quickly got back on track. You too, will find how to regain control of your life and probably learn things about yourself that you never knew.

By now, I'm certain you're mumbling something like, "that's fine for you, but I do not have a drinking problem". Take heart my dear ones. Clinics like this handle a whole range of emotional, mental, physical, sexual, verbal and other types of abuse, as well as drug and alcohol related issues. I didn't have a drinking problem either. Abuse was the problem, as it might be with you or someone you love. Remember, alcoholics, drug addicts or the abused are not bad people. They are basically good people with a bad disease or ugly emotional damage. Judging outward appearances is the first thing we have to dump. They are merely symptoms and we need to deal with the root cause. One of the leading contributors is uncontrolled anger. Here are some facts and figures just in case you think you are alone. You were simply one of many who were caught

The Alabaster Boy

up in an epidemic that has been sweeping this nation for years.

"Estimates range from 960,000 to 4,000,000 women who are physically abused by their husbands or live-in partners every year". *U.S. Department of Justice, March, 1998.* "Nearly one third of American women (31%) report being physically or sexually abused by a husband or boyfriend at some point in their lives".*Commonwealth Fund Survey, 1998.*

"The sad fact is that last year (2000), nearly a million children in the United States lived in homes filled with abuse and neglect. We can only guess at the actual numbers". * *Amarillo newspaper, April 2, 2001.*

"Studies show that child abuse occurs in 30-60% of family violence cases that involve families with children".*J.L. Edleson, Violence Against Women, February, 1999.*

"In 1996, among all female murder victims in the U.S., 30% were slain by their husbands or boyfriends". *Federal Bureau of Investigation, 1996.*

Joseph Anthony

"A child's exposure to the father abusing the mother is the strongest risk factor for transmitting violent behavior from one generation to the next". *Presidential Task Force on Violence and the Family, APA, 1996.*

"Family violence costs the nation from $5 to $10 billion annually in medical expenses, police and court costs, shelters and foster care, sick leave, absenteeism and non-productivity". *American Medical Association, January, 1992.*

Let's do the math and make it simple, shall we?

274,087,000 = U.S. population for the year 2000. * *U.S. Bureau of the Census*

116,218,000 females ages 16 + times 31% = 36,027,580 abused at some point.

97,555,000 males ages 16 + times 08% = 7,804,400 abused annually.

60,314,000 children ages 15 – times 30% = 13,149,594 abused at some point.

The Alabaster Boy

Amazing as it sounds, only 700,000 calls for assistance have been placed from February, 1996 to December, 2001. *National Domestic Violence Hotline report Of December, 2001.* That's wonderful, but that's a six year period and there have been at *least* 56,981,574 cases of abuse since 1996. How do we even begin to stem the tide of viciousness that has affected nearly 21% of our entire population? Obviously you start by calling and reporting. Those are the two biggest weapons we have against abuse. It would be a great idea to call before something happens, if you even suspect it will. Say this out loud to yourself until it is a reflex action: "I will ***call*** and ***report*** any incident".

In dire cases immediate help may have to come from the police and the court system. At the same time, a doctor of medicine should be consulted. You see abuse wears so many different faces and strikes so swiftly, that a *triage* method of treatment almost *has* to be used. First the most urgent physical needs must be dealt with. You simply cannot make rational decisions looking through eyes that have been beaten shut. Wounds must be treated. Next on the list would be a shelter or safe house for abused and battered women and children. It would be nice to see a few shelters for men!

After trauma has been relieved, a restraining order against the abuser is something you *must* obtain, or he will come around again, saying he is sorry and you'll forgive him…until next time. What if you don't make it to next time? Remember the FBI report on women murdered by their husbands or live-in partners? Are you going to be one of them? If you only believe one point in this book, believe this: In almost 100% of cases batterers/abusers *return* time after time, so you **must** call 911, get out of the home no matter what you have to do and have them arrested, despite the emotional ties. Remember *my* case. Abuse began on my wedding night and continued for 4 ½ years of marriage, plus 5 more years, until I moved from Indiana to Nevada. If you are still in the relationship, 'Getting Help: Safety Planning' is a matter of whether you live or die. * *The*

The Alabaster Boy

*National Coalition Against Domestic Violence **1(800) 799-SAFE (7233).***

1. Think of a safe place to go if an argument occurs – avoid rooms with no exits (bathroom), or rooms with weapons (kitchen).

2. Think about and make a list of safe people to contact.

3. keep change or a cell phone with you at all times.

4 Memorize or write down all important numbers and keep them on your person.

5. Establish a "code word or sign" so that family, friends, teachers or co-workers know when to call for help.

6. Think about what you will say to your partner if he/she becomes violent.

7. Remember you have the right to live without fear and violence

If you have left the relationship:

1. Change your phone number.

2. Screen phone calls.

3. Document and save all contacts, messages, injuries or other incidents involving the batterer.

4. Change locks if the batterer has a key.

5. Avoid staying alone.

6. Plan how to get away if confronted by an abusive partner.

7. If you have to meet your partner, do it in a public place and make sure it is not a bar. A drinking batterer will almost always attack, even in public. I have seen it happen.

8. Vary your routine.

9. Notify school and work contacts.

10. Call a shelter for battered women.

If you leave the relationship or are thinking of leaving, you should take important papers and documents with you to enable you to apply for benefits or take legal action. Important papers you should take with you include social security cards, certificates of birth for you and your children, marriage license, leases or deeds in your name or both your and your partner's names, your checkbook, your charge cards, bank statements, charge account statements, insurance policies, proof of income for you and your spouse (pay stubs or W-2's) and any documentation of past incidents of abuse (photos, police reports, medical records, etc.)

Counseling would be the next step, although you probably already will have received at least minimal counseling from the police, telling you the same things I just told you. Personally, I feel I need to warn, guard and protect you by emphasizing in the *strongest possible terms*, who to stay away from. After all, we are fragile and treatment is difficult enough without interference from a non-professional, good Samaritan who means well but can't really help you. The ones to avoid would be anyone not fully qualified to treat you. There are a lot of wanna-be people out there, carrying partial credentials, who are just itching to be called doctor, doctor, doctor, just because they have a PhD. So what! That degree only means Doctor of Philosophy. We're talking about abuse and that's real. It really hurts. Sometimes for years. Abuse is not something you *philosophize* away! Amateurs not only don't help, but can further injure, mistreat misdiagnose or even do irreparable damage. That's a horrifying thought, but it has happened before and will happen again, but hopefully not to you or any of your loved ones. In all fairness, there are multitudes of very good people out there with a lesser degree, who have the training and experience needed. They are most often associated with or working for a reputable and established clinic. If someone you show this to is offended, it's probably their ego and you should look elsewhere for help.

Group or individual (one on one) therapist or counselor, degreed social worker or counselor, psychologist, clinical psychologist and Doctor of Psychiatry is the general pecking order. All of these people are working toward the same goal, which is getting you any type of help you need to assist you in healing. My advice would be to try to get someone who has been through it all, then went through training and received a C.A.C. (Certified Addiction Counselor).

You might think you cannot afford this type of treatment, but it's cheaper than a hospital bill or a funeral. Most states and counties in this country offer abundant financial assistance that will cost you only a few bucks a visit compared to $135 and upwards.

Why should you seek help? The answer lies in what a man once said. "The definition of insanity is continuing to do what you've always done and expecting different results". * *unknown source* You are the one who needs to change things and you will. What can you expect from counseling and therapy? Something far better than you now have, such as becoming the real you by dumping all of those false guilt tags. Daring to discover feelings of inadequacy, real or imagined. Peeling off all of the masking devices you have put up to hide the demons of your shame and embarrassment.

Joseph Anthony

In the final analysis, walking out of the world of rape, verbal, sexual, physical and emotional abuse. Leaving the dungeon of despair, punishment and mental torment.

Living the life of a dignified human being. Realizing your role in the scheme of life. Recognizing and accepting your real potential. Truly acknowledging that you now have a much better chance to pursue and realize your dreams and goals.

Since anger is one of the leading causes of abuse, maybe you should be recognize the different forms it takes, how people use it and most importantly how to manage it instead of it controlling you or your loved ones. * *Northern Tier Counseling* : The Ten Faces of Anger are as follows:

1. Passive-Aggressive behavior
2. Caustic Remarks
3. Verbal Abuse
4. Blaming
5. Guerrilla Humor

6. Retaliatory Anger
7. Blind Rage
8. Isolation
9. Depression
10. Medicator

Seven ways people use anger * *Northern Tier Counseling*

As a buffer against feelings?

As a defense against shame?

An excuse?

Do you attack before you are attacked?

Does it give you a sense of power?

Does it allow you to feel righteously indignant?

Is it a high?

Only you know the answers. If these behavior patterns sound familiar maybe you need to learn and practice anger management, as I did. Please consider these seven basic steps: * *Northern Tier Counseling*

1. Admit we are angry and our lives have become problematic as a result of the destructive and unhealthy expression of anger.

2. Demonstrate a willingness to do something about your anger

3. Take a personal inventory of how your anger has affected your life.

4. Using a written inventory as a tool, admit to ourselves and to another human being, how it is you have been hurtful with your anger.

5. Make a written list of those you have harmed, yourself included and be willing to make amends.

6. Make direct amends to such people whenever possible, except when to do so would further injure them or others.

7. Continue to take a personal inventory of whether or not you are angry and when you are, promptly admit it.

The Alabaster Boy

One of my personal definitions might help to simplify all of these steps. Just understand that you can make your point without rage or anger. Aggressiveness is loud and angry, while assertiveness still lets you make your point, but without anger. That way you keep the same focal point, but it is now broken down into analysis. You can do it and feel a lot smarter and prouder of yourself. Getting angry is selfish because it is nothing more than instant gratification. Avoid it. Isn't that better than the Friday night fights?

"That's gonna' take too long", most would say, but *I* say, "Be not afraid of growing slowly. Be afraid only of standing still".

Another thing I've learned in my fifty seven years of living is that I have never done things I did *not* want to do. We all have choices. I've heard people say things like, "I *had* to get married". No you didn't. "She *made* me do it". No she didn't. "He made me do it". He didn't either. "I couldn't *help* eating an entire box of chocolates". Yes you could have. "I didn't *mean* to drive drunk". Yes you did. First you made a decision to drink. Then, with impaired judgment, you made a decision to get drunk. By then, you had no judgment, so you decided to drive. The bartender, your friends, spouse or the cops didn't make those decisions. You also chose to be arrested and go to jail the minute you made those few, faulty decisions back at the bar. "You don't see. It wasn't *my* choice".

Then whose choice was it? Those are all false concepts. In any situation you could have done what you knew was best. Instead, it was easier to go along with the program rather than to have the guts to say, "I don't want to and I won't, because it is not in my best interest". Doing things you have to do produces anger, frustration, inadequacy and makes you very upset. Make some good choices in things you *want* to do. Things you know are good for you. Those kinds of choices and actions build self esteem. The higher our self esteem, the more we are willing to risk. The more we succeed, the higher our self esteem. It's a continuous, positive

The Alabaster Boy

growth pattern that reassures us. We feel confident that we will make the correct choices, which will lead to a *want to life* instead of a *have to existence.*

Remember that in God's mind *you* are the most precious person on this planet. That makes *you* worthy. That makes *you* something special. *You* are *not* alone. There are men and women out there who are gentle and just as needy and sensitive as you and I. All of them would jump at the chance to love someone just like you!

ABOUT THE AUTHOR

Joseph Anthony began writing in 1992 by bringing memories of things he had experienced from his mind onto paper. Soon he was granted two syndicated columns in an east and west coast newspaper, which amounted to about 2 years of Sunday articles. Armed with experience, the author hungered to write more meaningful pieces. Thus, a ten year effort began and resulted in *The Alabaster Boy*. Critics say, "I couldn't put it down," "An emotional rollercoaster ride," "It leaves an indelible imprint" and "It is a life-transforming experience." Currently, this author continues to bare it all in more works. If as good as this book, you could be looking at a Pulitzer Prize winner.

EPILOGUE

"The woods are lovely, dark and deep,

But I have promises to keep

And miles to go before I sleep"

Robert Frost's 'To Earthward' – (1923)

Printed in the United States
53233LVS00001B